ONE
IS
A
CROWD

ONE

IS

A

CROWD

REFLECTIONS

OF AN

INDIVIDUALIST

FRANK CHODOROV

With an introduction by JOHN CHAMBERLAIN

THE DEVIN-ADAIR COMPANY, NEW YORK, 1952

HM
136
.C5

ACKNOWLEDGMENT

Some of the essays
in this book have previously
appeared in *Analysis;*
others in *Human Events,*
Faith and Freedom,
and *The Human Affairs Pamphlets,*
the last copyright by
Henry Regnery Company.
Still others appear for
the first time.

Book designed by Lewis F. White
Printed in the United States of America

DEDICATION

To Lisa and Eric
and their generation

INTRODUCTION

Along about 1935, in response to the so-called "challenge" of communism, America was blanketed by a literature of crypto-collectivism. There were neo-technocrats and "planners" by the score; the Keynesians and "middle way" journalists were out like night crawlers after a vesper shower. If numbers and the sort of thing that passes for intellectual journalism in this country were ever definitive, the cultural climate of our nation would have been altered beyond recall in those years. But one of the grand lessons of history is that you can not break the continuity of a culture or a tradition unless you are prepared to liquidate *all* those who have known the *douceur de la vie* of the old regime.

Lenin said it long ago: to make collectivism stick in a land that has known the blessings of individualism, you must catch a whole generation in the cradle and forcibly deprive it of tutors who have learned the bourgeois alphabet at their mothers' knees. In a land of republican law this is impossible; no matter how clever or omnipresent the collectivist propaganda may be, a few culture-carriers of the old tradition will escape. They may be reduced to publishing broadsheets instead of books; they may be compelled to conduct their straggling classes in dingy rooms in old brownstone fronts. Certainly they will have a hard time getting posts on a university faculty. But they will be still hanging around—and still talking—when the tinsel begins to wear off the latest Five-Year Plan or government-sponsored Greenbelt colonization scheme. Their books and pamphlets, ready for the chance encounter that sparks all revolutions or "reactions," will fan the revival of the old tradition that periodically displaces the callow presumptions of the "new."

A recent preoccupation with my own intellectual autobiography has led me to reflect on the culture-carriers who brought me back to what I had originally soaked up unconsciously in the individualistic New England of my childhood. One of these carriers was Albert Jay Nock, whose "Our Enemy the State" hit me between the eyes when I read it in the thirties. Another potent carrier was Franz Oppenheimer, whose concept of the State-as-racket (see his epochal book on "The State") was too formidably grounded in history to permit of any easy denial. Still another carrier was Garet Garrett, the only economist I know who can make a single image or metaphor do the work of a whole page of statistics. Then there was Henry George, the Single Taxer, and the Thoreau whose doctrine of civil disobedience implied a fealty to a higher—or a Natural—law, and Isabel Paterson, the doughty and perennially embattled woman who wrote "The God of the Machine." Finally, there was a man who sometimes spoke in parables and who always had a special brand of quiet humor, Mr. Frank Chodorov, whose lifetime of broadsheet writing and pamphleteering has been brilliantly raided by Devin A. Garrity of the Devin-Adair Co. to make this book.

Frank Chodorov is 65 years old, which means that he has been around. But he has the intellectual resilience that one would associate with the age brackets of the twenties and the thirties if the young of 1952 did not seem so frightened, so recessive, so pinched and so antique. The formal biography of Mr. Chodorov says that he once lectured at the Henry George School of Social Science; that he revived and edited *The Freeman* with Albert Jay Nock from 1938 to 1941 (*The Freeman* is one of those magazines that is always coming up

out of its own ashes, like the phoenix); that after one of the
intermittent deaths of *The Freeman* he published, wrote and
edited his own four-page monthly broadsheet called *analysis;* that he is currently engaged in editing *Human Events*
with Frank Hanighen in Washington, D. C.

A craftsman from the ground up, Frank Chodorov has
always made his own words pirouette with the grace and
fluidity of a Pavlova. Beyond this he is one of the few editors
alive who can make individual stylists of others merely by
suggesting a shift in emphasis here, an excision there, a bit
of structural alteration in the middle. To talk over the lunch-
eon table with Frank Chodorov about the problems of writing and editing is a liberal journalistic education. But this is
only the least important part of the education that one can
absorb from him when he is expanding in his own ruefully
humorous way.

Listening to Mr. Chodorov, you won't get any meaningless
gabble about "right" and "left," or "progressive" and "reac-
tionary," or liberalism as a philosophy of the "middle of the
road." Mr. Chodorov deals in far more fundamental distinctions. There is, for example, the Chodorovian distinction
between social power and political power. Social power de-
velops from the creation of wealth by individuals working
alone or in voluntary concert. Political power, on the other
hand, grows by the forcible appropriation of the individual's
social power. Mr. Chodorov sees history as an eternal struggle between social-power and political-power philosophies.
When social power is in the ascendant, men are inclined to
be inventive, creative, resourceful, curious, tolerant, loving
and good-humored. The standard of well-being rises in such
times—*vide* the histories of republican Rome, of the Hanse-
atic cities, of the Italian renaissance, of nineteenth century
Britain and of modern America. But when political power is
waxing, men begin to burn books, to suppress thought, and

to imprison and kill their dissident brothers. Taxation, which is the important barometer of the political power, robs the individual of the fruits of his energy, and the standard of life declines as men secretly rebel against extending themselves in labor that brings them diminishing returns.

According to the Chodorov rationale, *all* the great political movements of modern times are slave philosophies. For, no matter whether they speak in the name of communism, socialism, fascism, New Dealism or the Welfare (sometimes called the Positive) State, the modern political philosophers are all alike in advocating the forcible seizure of bigger and bigger proportions of the individual's energy. It matters not a whit whether the coercion is done by club or the tax agent —the coercion of labor is there; and such coercion is a definition of slavery. Nor does it matter that the energy-product of one individual is spent by the government on another: such spending makes beneficiaries into wards, and wards are slaves, too.

Mr. Chodorov is a mystic, but only in the sense that all men of insight are mystics. His mystical assumption is that men are born as individuals possessing inalienable rights. This philosophy of Natural Rights under the Natural Law of the Universe can not be "proved." But neither can the opposite philosophy—that Society has rights—be proved, either. You can say it is demonstrable that a State, as the police agent of Society, has power. But if there is no such thing as natural individual rights, with a correlative superstructure of justice organized to maintain those rights, then the individual has no valid subjective reason for obeying State power. True, the State can arrest the individual and compel his temporary obedience. But it can not compel his inner loyalty; nor can it keep men from cheating, or from the quiet withdrawal of energy. The rebellious individual can always find ways of flouting State power—which makes it dubious that Society (or the collectivity of men organized to compel individual men; has rights in any meaningful sense of the word. A collectivity can not have anything which its constitutive elements refuse to give up.

Since the human animal must make either one mystical assumption or another about rights, Mr. Chodorov chooses the assumption that accords with the desire of his nature, which is to protect itself against the lawlessness of arbitrary power. He is mystical in the same way that James Madison and Thomas Jefferson and the rest of the Founding Fathers were mystical; and he is religious enough to believe in Nature's God, which is to say that he believes in Natural Law.

The utilitarian argument is that Natural Law does not apply in the field of ethics, since it is not demonstrable that a thief will always be caught and punished, or a murderer apprehended, or a polygamist forced to relinquish his extra wives. But if there is no Natural Law of Ethics, then any system of ethics is as valid as the next—and the choice of fascism or cannibalism is no "worse" than the choice of freedom as defined by John Locke. Mr. Chodorov's answer to the utilitarians is that men are diminished and blighted under certain ethical systems, whereas they flourish under other systems. And it is demonstrably the nature of man to prefer life to death, or to the slow agony of death-in-life that goes with slave systems.

Mr. Chodorov never labors his principles in either his writing or his speaking. Nor does he indulge in debater's tricks. He prefers a good parable to formal argument, and he is at his best when he is raiding the Old Testament to make a modern point. His essay on "Joseph, Secretary of Agriculture," which is a simple recapitulation, with Chodorovian "asides," of the Old Testament story of Joseph and the Ever Normal Granary, tells us all we want to know about Henry Wallace and the Brannan Plan. This essay is first-rate entertainment. But it is also good instruction; like all good teachers, Chodorov knows that instruction is always improved when it comes in the form of entertainment. What he offers in his essays as entertainment is, of course, worth ten of the ordinary political science courses that one gets in our modern schools. It is a measure of our educational delinquency that nobody has ever seen fit to endow Mr. Chodorov with a university chair. But his successors will have chairs once Mr. Chodorov has completed his mission in life, which is to swing the newest generations into line against the idiocies of a collectivist epoch that is now coming to an end in foolish disaster and blood.

JOHN CHAMBERLAIN

CONTENTS

CHAPTER 1

ON PROMOTING

INDIVIDUALISM

I was talking to a group of deplorers. There is no dearth of them these days, what with the national passion for pushing power on the government. This group, however, was most concerned with the spread of collectivistic bilge in our schools and colleges. Of a certainty, what we are getting in the way of legislation and propaganda is the result of what has been learned and is being taught. It follows that any change in the direction of both legislation and public thought must begin with education. Something had to be done about it.

One man suggested the establishment of a College of Individualism, as a sort of intellectual powerhouse to feed ideas to other disseminators. Innocently, I asked the question: what is individualism? I was aiming at a curriculum.

1

There was a good deal of floundering, as I had antici-pated. In politics—we were sure of that—individualism is a negative point of view: cut government to the bone. But, what is the allowable minimum? The downright anarchist was for abolishing all government, on the premise that peo-ple would improve morally by its absence; the majority al-lowed that a traffic cop is a social need.

In economics, all of us accepted the general line of thought laid down by Adam Smith, though one man de-clared Smith's ideas on free trade impractical under present world conditions, and that brought on a heated argument. A theologian in the group insisted that individualism is pri-marily a spiritual concept, and if that were set straight the rest of the curriculum would take care of itself.

The curriculum, one bold voice suggested, is of minor im-portance; the faculty is the thing. Whatever subject an indi-vidualist handles, he maintained, he cannot help but bring his values to bear upon it; just as a collectivist, teaching biol-ogy, cannot refrain from comparing the innards of a frog with the organization of the State. The thing to do, then, is to pack the faculty with dyed-in-the-wool individualists and let each formulate his own course. The students would get a full dose of individualism whatever they studied.

This idea posed a new question: what is an individualist? Is he born or made? Socialism laughs at the theory of innate characteristics and insists that we come into this world with-out temperamental shape; men can be turned by environ-ment, including education, this way or that. Yet, the constant recurrence of the rebel is an historical refutation of this Socialistic thesis, and every mother of more than one child will bear witness against it. Some of us conform easily, others find it necessary to question every existing conven-tion. Perhaps psychology could furnish us with an explana-tion of the individualist; or, of the socialist.

If individualism is not an acquired characteristic, but is grounded in one's personality, what can education do about it? Nothing more than to give articulation to what the student already feels. For instance, if he instinctively finds regulation repugnant, he will be helped no end by an understanding of the doctrine of natural rights; conversely, if he is a regimenter at heart, he will rationalize that doctrine into a myth. The purpose of teaching individualism, then, is not to make individualists but to find them. Rather, to help them find themselves. If a student takes readily to such values as the primacy of the individual, the free market place, or the immorality of taxation, he is an individualist; if he swallows hard, he must be counted a recruit for the other side.

At this point, someone brought up a current phenomenon: the increasing number of deserters from the Communist camp. If these recanters came to Communism by natural selection, how could they throw it off? Or, did they? Is an intellectual conversion capable of purging an innate inclination?

The books written by these "exes" give a clue to the answer. One does not get from their confessions of sin, or exposés of Soviet skulduggery, the idea that the authors are done with collectivism. Their sneering references to capitalism indicate that they are of the same opinion still. Communism, they will admit, is Socialism gone hog-wild, but they do not seem capable of recognizing this as an inevitable consequence. Their hatred of Communism does not make them individualists.

This is not to question the sincerity of those who have hit the sawdust trail. Far from it. The individualist, who accepts as basic the right of every man to make a fool of himself— provided he does not infringe the equal rights of others—is quick to accept the repentance at face value. But, repentance is not conversion; there is reason to believe that conversion is impossible.

The "right-wing" socialist is another case in point. The hatred he harbors for Communism is intense, but only because he looks upon it as treason. He condemns Stalin and his crowd because they have, forsooth, betrayed the Marxist ideal. In the hands of good and true Socialists—right-wingers, of course—the Russian "experiment" of 1918 would by now have come up with a shining demonstration of the Socialist promise. No amount of logic can convince him that the only possible result of Marxism in practice is Russia, as is.

Coming to the garden variety of collectivist—the do-gooder, who differs from the socialist only in that he substitutes sentimental clichés for "scientific" Socialism—he too seems psychologically incapable of letting people alone. He too is inexorably bent on hammering out the Good Society on the political anvil. He too has the perfect recipe, an ingredient of which is his own capacity for improving others. It is endemic.

All the evidence points to the collectivist as a breed, not a product. Which is also true of the individualist. The main characteristic of the one is an urge to ride herd on mankind, while the other is inclined to give mankind a wide berth. The collectivist idealizes group behavior because he feels an inadequacy in himself; he must be part of a mob and therefore he organizes and joins. The individualist abhors labels.

The volume of sound generated by the organized collectivist gives him undue prominence. He seems to be the majority. Yet, if nature is as impartial in the distribution of temperaments as she is in the apportionment of sexes, there should be as many individualists around as the other kind. Nor can we overlook the possibility that all of us have a penchant both ways, being part individualist and part collectivist, in differing degrees; one could adduce evidence in favor of that thesis.

Only education can give the right answer; for the function of education is to bring to the surface what nature has implanted in the person. If the educational machinery of the country had not been overrun by the collectivists (operating under cover of "academic freedom"), if individualism were given a fair share of the curriculum, we could easily find out how many of us prefer freedom, how many of us are destined to be mob material.

Returning to our group of deplorers, we got around to the need of stirring up an interest in the individualistic philosophy on the college campus. To be sure, we knew that the younger children were being subjected to the cacophony of collectivism, and a thorough job of saving must include the lower grades, even the kindergarten. But, immediacy suggested throwing a lifeline to adolescent individualists, those who will have a hand in shaping the world directly ahead.

As a *modus operandi,* we thought of encouraging the formation of what we called Adam Smith Clubs. This would have to be an extracurricular activity, for two reasons: one, the monopolization of the classroom by the faculty collectivists is too solid to permit penetration; two, these clubs would pick up, by a process of self-selection, the element susceptible of help.

Suppose it were noised about that at the next meeting of the club, a speaker would hold forth on the iniquity of the income tax, or would expose the fraud of social security; those who instinctively rejected the textbook apotheoses of these two institutions would attend, while the energumens of collective action would stay away, especially if they had once felt the uncongenial atmosphere. Every Adam Smith Club would be a campus "educable elite."

On the face of it, an Adam Smith Club would be an evidence of a dissident voice on the campus and, considering the vogue of Keynesianism and pragmatism in our colleges, it would be looked upon with disfavor by the vested collectivists and campus conformists. All the better. Any explicit or implicit opposition to the Club would convince the membership that they had got hold of an important truth. It is a known fact that the learning one acquires outside the lecture hall sticks closer to the ribs, especially if that learning is officially declared off limits.

It would be a pity if the Adam Smith Clubs achieved respectability; that woud destroy their purpose. Their purpose should be not only to find and help the submerged individualist, but also to set him in opposition to the collectivism being ladled out by the professors. A compromise is impossible; it is a fight to the finish. The agenda of the meetings should include the preparation of refutations of textbook propaganda, to be fired in classroom, with the intent of stirring up latent individualists. If the Adam Smith Clubs are to be really educational, they must be radical in character.

For, it must be kept in mind that individualism is the modern radicalism. In the true sense of the word, individualism is always radical, for it rests its case on root ideas; it delves into the nature of things for basic causes; it rejects the idea that man is best served by a series of expedients.

In the political sense, individualism is the current radicalism because it is the ideology of the minority. The ultimate purpose of the Adam Smith Clubs should be to loosen the grip of Statism on the mass mind, to re-arouse in America an awareness of self-importance and self-reliance, to teach people that no social good can come out of politics.

There are, as a matter of fact, incipient Adam Smith Clubs on some campuses. The individualist simply cannot be eradicated. In every period of history when the machinery of the

State, including education, was set against him, he made his spirit felt. It is not surprising, therefore, to hear of the spontaneous gathering of anti-collectivists at various colleges. These boys and girls should be given encouragement and help. And that would be the purpose of a College of Individualism.

CHAPTER 2

HOW A JEW
CAME TO GOD

An Intellectual Experience

 AM a Jew. Not that anyone cares, least of all myself, and my abrupt declaration serves only to introduce the story of an intellectual experience, not a sermon nor anything suggestive of a purpose. My excuse for bringing the matter up at this time is that there is some talk about a "Jewish problem," and the recrudescence of this phrase, with its socially unpleasant connotations, has again got me to asking myself what it is that I am when I name myself, or am named, a Jew. For the better part of a half century I have tried to capture the invariable positives and negatives of the human being so labelled, but, so far, my intellectual curiosity has not been answered. I admit that this curiosity was whetted on the emery wheel of unpleasant experiences, but it is still lively after the years have turned these experiences into pleasant reminiscences.

Maybe I would have forgotten the whole thing if some people who call themselves Christian, which defies definition almost as stubbornly, did not make it their business to re-fasten the label on me whenever through forgetfulness I have allowed the edges to become loose. They seemed to care a great deal more than I do. And they show their concern in ways that are often ingenious and with a sense of delicacy; and sometimes they are not so nice about it. There's the fellow who explains, when he invites me to lunch, that he is not taking me to his club—I did not know he belonged to one—because "there's a stupid feeling among the members, which of course I do not share, that might prove embarrassing, and I wouldn't have that for all the world." Or the one who in a complimentary mood assures me that I am not a Jew but "like one of us." And the cliché "some of my best friends are Jews" is definitely used to properly place me. Thus, by innuendo, inference or direct statement, or even a knowing look, I am gratuitously reminded that I am what I am whenever the fact slips my mind. All my years I have been called, and have called myself, a Jew, and that, according to some authorities, establishes the fact. But, the question will not down, what do these three letters describe or define? I've asked the question of many people and have got almost as many different answers, not one of which squares with observable fact.

Subjectively, I know that "I am"; but as for "a Jew," I have no consciousness of it at all. It has never been revealed to me; I have learned it by rote only. Hunger, fatigue, headache and itch are quite real. There is no mistaking these facts of consciousness. But never have I experienced a similar perception of Jewishness. There may be people to whom

perceptions of race, religion or nationality are as definite as
the taste of ice cream, but I am inclined to believe that these
ideas are like lipstick or a coat—something one puts on and
takes off. Or has put on, like shackles. Be that as it may, I am
devoid of any sensory perception of Jewishness.

A Lexicographer's Search

I look into the mirror and see there the reflection of features similar to those worn by others called Jews. Yes, my
face has a marked resemblance to my father's, also to my
brothers', and my children bear the same features. Maybe,
then, there are certain distinctions of physiognomy which,
if they could be captured in words, would settle this matter
of definition. However, I observe features quite suggestive
of my own worn by people who are not called Jews; the ex-
clusiveness becomes uncertain. My people came from Russia,
and I notice that many Russian Christians, on the basis of
their facial characteristics, could easily pass for blood relations. Then I see Jews with straight, thin noses, dark skins
and slender contours, features usually associated with Latin
peoples; the Jewish girl I married was sometimes taken for a
Spaniard. Again, there is the hooked proboscis of the German Jew which is equally characteristic of the Aryan faces.
The search for a definition must go beyond features.

I said my people came from Russia, from the southern
part, around Odessa. In the eighth and ninth centuries that
part of the world was occupied by a pagan people known as
the Khazars. The record classifies them as Tartars, but as the
territory embraced a transit between the Black Sea and the
Caspian, there is some doubt as to the singleness of their
blood, for in all probability it was tainted with Persian, Hun,
Armenian, Slavonic and whatever other kind came down
this path of war and trade. Now, legend has it that many of

these Khazars were converted to Judaism; some say the entire tribe was. Can it be, then, that far back among my progenitors I could find an adulterated Tartar? Perish the thought! Yet we know that marriage is a matter of propinquity, not of race; and if the Russian Jew bears a likeness to his Christian compatriot, the idea of consanguinity cannot be put away. Taking into consideration the fact of biological transmission of physical characteristics, can we not say that in his matings the Jewish male, like all other males, has not been scrupulously race-conscious? And Jewish girls are not hard to look at either. But, why belabor the point? Solomon, we are told, had three hundred wives and a thousand concubines. He picked them for their beauty only, and he went far and wide to get them. So, we Jews got pretty well mixed up with non-Jews long, long before the dispersion, and have been as continuously guilty of intermarriage as the people we intermarried with. It seems, then, that a racial definition, in the sense of a continuous stream of the same kind of blood, will hardly hold.

Well, then, how about a definition based on religion? And the rejoinder is, which Jewish religion are you talking about? A while ago I was reading about the ritual in the Holy Temple at the time of Pontius Pilate and it occurred to me that a reincarnated high priest of the times would find himself more at home at a Catholic high mass than in the modern temple of the "better class" Jew. Imagine the mortification of a bewhiskered and skull-capped Polish Jew in the house of worship frequented by his hatless son, where the women's chests are exposed and where no rail or elevation separates the sexes. It's as much as to ask him to eat pork chops— which the son does. In proportion to their numbers, the Jews can probably lay claim to as many schisms as do the Christians, to say nothing of the many who own up to no sect.

Then there is the attempt to give the Jews a nationalistic definition.* If I adhere to this idea I say to myself: I am part of a political entity which lost its physical reality some two thousand years ago; this nation exists in the record of its past, its cultural continuity and in its well-advertised manifest destiny. It is a nation without the physical appurtenances of one. Examining that fancy, I ask myself, can two thousand years of history be wiped out, as if it never happened? What warrant have we in nature for the persistence of national entities? Has not every state carved out its career with the sword, and when that sword lost its edge did not the state disappear? It is interesting to read about the ancient Greeks, to study the records of Aztec culture or the unearthed artifacts of lost empires. I would like to know why these social integrations disappeared, why such highly developed civilizations could not maintain themselves. Such information might help me foretell the course of the civilization of which I am a part. But I feel no call to fight for the restoration of a state which exists only in poetry. Citizenship in a state without authority is a contradiction. Furthermore, the ideology involved in the proposed restoration smacks too much of Hitlerian nationalism based on racial purity, reinforced with claims to divine selection. It defies the record and is decidedly dangerous.

* This was obviously written before the advent of Israel. The argument is still the same. This new state, despite the arguments of professional Zionists, is by no means a continuation or revival of the one ruled by Solomon or Caesar. It is brand new, and I feel no more attachment to it than I do for the one that is presumed to be its predecessor. There is a strident group in this country who insist that American citizenship does not absolve the Jew from loyalty to Israel, that he is in fact vested with dual citizenship, the stronger of which, judging by their demands for financial help, is in the newly acquired half. That is silly. In the event of conflict between Israel and the United States (not an impossibility, since geography might compel Israel into the U.S.S.R. camp), which of his two loyalties would lay first claim on him? Or, perchance, would he take up arms against himself? . . . However, if loyalty to Israel is the identification of a Jew, then I declare unequivocally that I am not one.

And so it has been all these years. An examination of the
suggested definitions amounts to a process of elimination,
and it is not surprising that mysticism is resorted to by many;
accordingly, the Jew is endowed with a soul which is *sui
generis* and undefinable. Maybe so. But I confess to an in-
capacity in such supersensory perceptibility. When things
get beyond the rational I am lost. . . . And so, I have come
to the conclusion that I am a Jew because I call myself one,
and so does everybody else who cares to classify me, and
that is all there is to it. I have hit upon a description of the
Jew which, while lacking the conciseness of a definition,
helps to identify his particularism. We'll go into that after
I have got along with my story.

Early Background

The lower west side of New York at the turn of the century
was going through the usual transition of a fine residential
section into an area of low-priced tenements, rooming houses
and marginal factories. The street where I spent my pre-high
school days was already entering the factory phase. A few
streets away the vestiges of early New York aristocracy held
on to its brownstone elegance; that was nearly twenty years
before enterprising realtors rescued these anachronisms from
well-deserved demolition. They painted the fronts white
and the shutters green, and invested the section with profitable romance by reviving its ancient name of Greenwich
Village. I never heard the name when I went to school in
that section.

There were two Jewish families besides mine in the neigh-
borhood, and one moved uptown before I got to high school.
Irish, French and Italian emigrants had taken over, sometimes creating distinct nationalistic islands on contiguous
streets, sometimes getting all mixed up as they did on my
street. Much to the chagrin of my mother, my associates were

not only not of my people, but were inclined to practices not sanctioned by the *Talmud* or any other moral code. The only reason I did not accompany some of my companions to the reformatory was that I was not apprehended in the business of selling lead pipe purloined from partially built or empty houses.

One had to fight to live in this environment and the "Jew" epithet was as good a *casus belli* as any other. But, the matter rarely came up in a purely descriptive form, the viciousness of the accompanying adjectives rather than the word itself being the real challenge. I was yet to learn the flavor of real anti-Semitism. The fact that I didn't go to church on Sunday marked me off, but I recall being envied for that good fortune. I could and would fight, I was good at the games we played, and when the gang had some collective purpose to pursue I was expected to do my share. Race consciousness never entered into our affairs.

I knew I was a Jew. There was no question about that but it did not bother me. It did bother my mother, of course. She had a rabbi come to the house to teach me Hebrew. My apostasy began right there and then, not only because this added education interfered with my ball games, but also because of my objections to the pedagogical method of the rabbi. He insisted on my learning Hebrew by sight and sound, rather than by understanding of the text, and progress was made difficult by my impertinent interrogations. I began to suspect that these hieroglyphics hid objectionable ideas.

An incident of this period did much to undermine whatever inclination I may have had toward the ancient tradition. One very cold night the rabbi tottered into our house in a pitiful condition; it took a half dozen glasses of boiling tea to thaw him out. He then told how a sympathetic "goy" had offered him a pair of gloves and why he had refused the gift; a Jew must not be the instrument of bringing a "mit-vah," or blessing, on a non-believer. That was the first time, I believe, that I came smack up against the doctrine of the "chosen people," and it struck me as stupid and mean.

The real and permanent education of the child consists in the fermentation of ideas put into its mind by experience; against that all book learning is as nothing. For instance, I remember well my last trip to the synagogue, when I was eleven years of age, on Yom Kippur. The ritual was of an-cient vintage; women and children worshipped in the bal-cony, while the shoeless, shawled and skull-capped men on the main floor faced the walls as they incanted the prayers to the metronomic swaying of their bodies. Not all of the men followed custom so meticulously, but the more devout could be so identified. One of these attracted my attention because he was head of the other Jewish family on the street. This fellow came by a bad reputation in the community, for shady business practices, for uncouthness and loudness, for wife-beating. My folks were hardly on speaking terms with this man or his family. Well, on this particular holy day our neighbor was doing his devotions with noticeable intensity, and that started me thinking and asking questions. Could one day of hard prayer in a synagogue wash out the sins of a whole year? Is God bought off so cheaply? My mother par-ried me for a while and then brushed me off with "the ways of God must not be questioned." That settled it. I sneaked off to an important one-o'-cat game on the street.

My mother finally got her wayward son into high school. These four years were indeed happy ones. Contact with boys of more reputable background weaned me away from docks, warehouses, gang warfare and trial by fisticuffs. Football helped to reflate the ego which had somewhat collapsed in this more rarefied atmosphere; the acclaim of the crowd on Saturday afternoons was reassuring. I began to take a more

than perfunctory interest in books. I even became conscious
of marks. I took part in extra-curricular activities other than
athletics, such as the school paper and a literary society, and
all in all enjoyed high school immensely. During these years
not once, as far as I can recall, did the matter of discrimination make itself felt.

Higher Learning

Then came college. To me matriculation was quite an experience, almost a hallowed event. In those days most boys
who went to college did so because that was in the tradition
of their class and matriculation was like the first shave, something one did because one had arrived. Boys of my world
almost always completed their formal education at fourteen,
a few more put in four years of high school (or less, if circumstances demanded), and a smaller number whose
parents were ambitious for them got to college. Higher education was hard to come by; only those who showed special
ability, as evidenced in competitive examinations, were sub-
sidized. Society had not yet taken on the collective duty of
raising its moronic level. Hence, for those of us who were
determined to "work our way through" the mere fact of having entered was an exhilarating experience.

Nothing happened during the first few weeks to indicate
that social life in college would be much different from what
it was in high school. I went out for football, fully confident
that I would make the grade. In my relations with the squad
I was diffident, not because of any race consciousness, but
because I felt out of place in an atmosphere where tradition
counted. I was a bit afraid of it. In high school this lack was
brought home to me in a poignant way. Through our mutual
interest in literature another lad and I struck up a close ac-
quaintanceship, and one afternoon he invited me to dine

with his folks. It was not the quiet elegance of the home that
most impressed me, although that was considerably different
from the utilitarian surroundings I associated with home.
What struck me with force was the easy courtesy that graced
the relationship between my friend, his older brother and
their mother. It wasn't manners, it was manner. This was all
new to me and I was filled with fear that I might prove myself out of place. Particularly so when the two boys came to
dinner dressed in their dinner-coats (which I believed were
worn only at class and fraternity dinners); in not the slightest way was I made conscious of my non-conformity. I
learned then that in social deportment the docks had taught
me little.

A few such experiences put me on my guard. I played
hard and left the matter of companionship to the others, ex-
pecting it to come when I proved myself. One thing annoyed
me. In those days of interlocking interference the ball carrier was part of the ball, and interferers were expected to
pull, push or throw him for an extra foot or inch. But, nary a
hand touched me. I did not understand it, and must have
shown my confusion, for one day the only other Jewish boy
on the squad said to me, "Don't let it get you, kid; it's tough
going for a Jew on this squad, but you've got what it takes
and you'll make good." So, that's what it was! It was my first
introduction to the finesse with which discrimination could
be practiced.

My education along these lines progressed rapidly. I had
played in all the freshman games, was considered a first-
stringer and fully expected to "win my numerals" in the final
game. When the coach called out the starting line-up in the
locker-room just before game time, my name was not on the
list, and nobody seemed to think it odd. I did, of course.
What hurt me the most was that there was no way of openly

resenting the affront, without being churlish, and the best I could do was to take it out on the opposing players when necessity compelled the coach to put me into the game.

The open attack—the "goddam Jew"—came one Friday afternoon. The varsity coach—we had no rule barring freshmen those days—kept me for special instruction; I was being taught the fine art of throwing my body into mass plays, and for that purpose a skeleton offense was opposed to me. On the very first rehearsal I felt a fist on my jaw. It happened again, and the third time the epithet was thrown with the fist. Whatever polish I had acquired in the past few years left me completely, and with the choicest language of my past I sailed into the senior to whom I traced the offense. To my chagrin, he wouldn't fight. I thought later that the whole thing may have been a prearranged affair, to test my toughness, for the next day I was put into the varsity game. But at the time I was burned up.

There were other incidents, on the field and on the campus. One that sticks in my memory after all these years occurred about three months after the start of the term. A fellow with whom I had been very friendly at high school, a member of my fraternity there, passed me as I was crossing the campus with another friend, without acknowledging my salutation. I said to my companion: "What's the matter with Carl, is he deaf?" "No, not deaf, but didn't you see that fraternity pledge pin on his lapel? He can't be friendly with a Jew now." That hurt.

Soon I learned that discrimination was not confined to the students. Some of the Jewish upper-classmen protested openly against the wave of anti-semitism that year—I learned later that it was a regular autumnal phenomenon—and were for doing something about it. They called a meeting. I would have laughed at such a thing in high school; but I went to this one. That is something the persecutors do not understand—that persecution makes a minority: as the professional Jews well know, if Jews are unmolested they tend to lose all sense of commonality and go their separate ways; they coalesce in proportion to the pressure put upon them. At this meeting a committee was appointed to consult with a Jewish professor, a man of international repute, on ways and means. "Forget it," advised the professor, "and it will die down. Let me tell you something. We Jewish members of the faculty are invited to all faculty functions, but we always decline, because we are expected to decline."

A Mission Is Born

By the end of my freshman year I had about soured on college life. Being husky and pugnacious, I found relief in fisticuffs, whenever the opportunity presented itself, which was rare, because the affronts were subtle and intangible; I don't doubt that sensitiveness found slights where none were intended. It occurred to me later that if I had developed in my earlier years a sense of comradeship with Jews as Jews, adjustment to this new world would not have gone so hard. I could have eased into the discrimination rather than have it pounded into me. I realized, too late, that I would have done better by myself if I had not ventured into the sacred temple of footballism. One is never hurt if one keeps one's place. It must have been particularly difficult for the rich Jewish boys who tried to buy their way into forbidden social circles and were despised for it by their own kind, as well as by the others.

Beginning with my sophomore year I went to college for the sole purpose of learning a trade, and learning it as fast as possible. So, in spite of the necessity of earning enough to pay my tuition, I took on sufficient subjects, and one summer course, to cut my college career by one year. But, peculiarly enough, my hard introduction into anti-semitism blossomed into a purpose; I would try to find the cause for this horrible thing and see what could be done about eradicating it. Toward that end I selected from the electives as much philosophy as was allowed to an undergraduate. This idea came to me, I think, from the numerous references to God and religion which I ran across in a text book used in one of the philosophy courses; I had already come to the *a priori* conclusion that religion was at the bottom of social discords. Maybe, then, philosophy would help me solve the riddle.

I remember particularly a course in the history of philosophy. The sessions were held late in the afternoon for the convenience of students from the theological seminary. There were also some older students, specials, with heretical tendencies, and only the diplomatic skill of the professor prevented the metaphysical battles from becoming brawls. The post-session arguments in the corridors provided the real fun of the course; and here the athiests had the best of it, probably because they were more emphatic. The sharpest of these was a Jew, a special student about thirty years of age, whose deep sincerity indicated that he had a mission. Before the year was up the God-less ones had me on their side, and I had a mission too. An emotional experience had given my intellectual groping a definite direction.

There was no doubt in my mind that I had found "truth." Having found it, I was in no mood for further questioning, for contemplative reflection. All I needed now was confirmation of my discovery, for which I looked to propaganda. I swallowed whole the agnosticism of Robert Ingersoll and the "Age of Reason" became my bible against the Bible. The anti-clerical tales with which seventeenth and eighteenth century literature is full served as documentary proof of the perfidy of all things religious. Atheistic literature and a publication, for which I later wrote an article or two, fed me with phrases that served for reason. It is easy to found a philosophy upon a half-truth, the easiest thing in the world of thought. The anti-semitism which had hurt me became only a single expression of the evil which religion had always wrought, and I linked the sufferings of the Jews with the slaughter of the Hugenots, the massacre of Christians by the followers of Mohamet, the Inquisition and all the persecutions that throughout history had been done in the name of God. The Borgias can be explained psychologically or politically; I chose to explain them as the product of religious mania. Whenever I read of slaughter in the name of "God and country" I blamed it on God alone. Religion became the cause of all strife, the church the altar upon which human happiness is sacrificed, clericalism the embodiment of all evil. The world would never be a fit place to live in until the whole kit and kaboodle were wiped out. And toward that wind-mill I tilted my lance.

I sometimes wonder whether reformers are more interested in their egos than their reforms. My judgement in the matter would be biased. At any rate, I think I was quite sincere in my anti-God crusade. I sought converts. In Chicago —where I was employed as an advertising man, having given up as hopeless for a Jew the ambition of becoming a professor of English—there was an institution known as the "nut club." Membership was voluntary, unpaid, and the meetings were held in a park. Every warm evening or weekend men bent on impressing their views on one another would proceed to do so without formality. Two arguers would lock horns and if they tussled well a crowd would gather about them. No parliamentary rules and very few rules of courtesy impeded the progress of the debate. Hour upon hour this would continue, with new protagonists taking the place of the exhausted ones. This "nut club" was just what I needed to develop my enthusiasm and I was a regular member, the protests of my young wife notwithstanding. I was loyal to my atheism.

More Education

About eight years after I left college I ran across a book I had heard something about and had put down on my reading list. It was *Progress and Poverty*. A friend had a copy in his library—he said he had never read it—and while waiting for him to shave I read the introduction entitled *The Problem*. It explored the age-old social problem of poverty in the midst of plenty and promised the reader an inquiry into the cause. I wasn't particularly interested in the proposition, although my contact with poverty should have predisposed me to it, but was struck with the literary style. Here was something of the cameo clarity of Matthew Arnold, a little of the parallel structure of Macaulay, the periods of Edmund Burke, and with all this Victorianism a new-world fervor that was catching. I know I was more interested in how this man Henry George—some fellow who, I had heard, had run for mayor of New York—said it than in what he had to say. Probably a nineteenth century essayist, I surmised, whom I had missed and the deficiency had to be made up. I borrowed the book for a week or two.

For six months I read and re-read this book, even to the neglect of the "nut club." Some technicalities in economics delayed my progress, and a rather involved discussion of the nature of interest came near flooring me. There were too, occasional panegyrics about God and the natural order which I passed off as nineteenth century flubdubbery with which the author sugar-coated his decidedly radical ideas. Through it all there was a cogency in the reasoning that could not be denied. I became convinced the author had something.

And then came a thought which disturbed my enthusiasm. If Mr. George was right, that poverty and the fear of it stir up social hatreds, then bigotry is a mere manifestation and organized religion is not a basic cause. That tended to upset the case I had built up. Suppose, I said to myself, I were to level all the churches, put the priesthood out of business, convince everybody that religion is poison, there would still be the problem of poverty; there would still be an environment that makes for tough boys and another that produced dinner-coated young gentlemen. And maybe, I continued, the troubles which I had been laying at the door of the conniving pious is in fact the product of poverty, as Mr. George claimed. Well, at any rate, there were now two strings to my bow, economics and religion, and I could vary my diatribes, just for a change.

I tried out my newly acquired theory in the park. The defense of an idea begets conviction of its correctness. Even before I knew the answers I managed to parry questions with plausibilities which, strangely enough, I frequently found corroboration for in the book, to which I had to refer often. The crowd seemed to be much more interested in this poverty-in-the-midst-of-plenty argument than in attacks on the institution of religion, and it might be that this greater interest had some influence on my intellectual switch; even a crusader likes to please a crowd, and, in fact, likes a crowd to please. I gradually gave up on religion and put my reading time to economics and social problems. These were subjects I had paid little attention to at college; now they seemed all-important and I began reading all I could find on them, including, of course, the other books of Henry George. The thread of piety which ran through his works I dismissed for years as so much persiflage. Finally, and reluctantly, it dawned on me that his religious concepts in some way integrated his economics and his social philosophy. His God and

his natural law meant something to his scheme of thought
and I determined to find out what it was, even though, having been scorched by pragmatism as well as agnosticism, I
was sure there was nothing to it.

What About "Natural Rights"?

I found in the writings of Mr. George frequent references
to the idea of absolute right. Upon reflection, it occurred to
me that though this idea is definitely metaphysical I had
been relying upon it, without question, in my quarrel with
anti-semitism. It is the principle enunciated in the Declaration of Independence, that in their public relations all people must be accounted equal, that none have an inherent
claim to prerogatives as against the others. But why?
Whence comes the authority for this principle? It is not a
legal matter, since the implication is quite clear that the
business of the law, in theory at least, is merely to implement
this inherent quality. It is a law above the law, of an invariable which men may not affect even though they ignore it
to their detriment. Nor is this principle a matter of expediency in social relations, as the pragmatists claim, since on
the ground of expediency argument could well be adduced
for the suspension of equality; as when a nobility or a political party promote their own ascendancy "for the general
good."

The Declaration finds authority for this principle of equality in a Creator. Here the human mind, finding no other
answer to its eternal "why," takes recourse to its imagination
and invents a first cause. The atheist rejects this concept as a
myth, the agnostic says "I don't know." But both of them, in
attacking the evil practices of organized religion, look to the
"nature of things" for a moral yardstick. Everybody who
objects to injustice does so on the ground that these practices violate some principle of justice which is above human

will. This is so even when authority for justice, or equality among men, is found in the "dignity of the individual"; for that phrase is just as metaphysical as the "nature of things."

Reasoning so, I recognized that in spite of my pragmatic leanings I too had unconsciously premised my social thinking on the assumption of a "natural order." I saw that this assumption is the essence of religious thinking, and I reflected how every social philosophy with which I was familiar likewise fell back on an extra-human pattern of things. Even the ultra-materialistic socialists, in their doctrine of historical inevitability, are guilty of transcendentalism. Admittedly, I reasoned, this is a flight of the finite mind from its own limitations; it is a search for security in an invariable; it is mining for bedrock in the infinite; and in so doing it must rely on its power of imagination. It does so as a matter of necessity. It must "make sense" of the world in which it lives, since it revolts at the madness induced by chaos. If it rejects the principle of essential equality among men, which admittedly it finds only in the myth of the "natural order," the human mind is led logically into a mess of incongruities. Thus, if all men are not created equal, what objection could one make to a master-and-slave status? That a few enjoy wealth and power at the expense of the many should occasion no quarrel, since it just happened so and there is no warrant in reason for disturbing the arrangement. Exploitation, discrimination or social disabilities of any kind do not exist if the premise of parity is false. The only justification for a change in the status would be the force one could apply toward that end. Rejection of any concept of absolute right makes justice synonymous with power, and that is an incongruity the mind finds difficult to accept. In this flight from such madness the human mind finds haven in logical fiction.

I found, then, that I had built my whole case against minority disabilities on an article of faith. And there was no way of getting away from it. Whichever way I turned the argument for equality I came to the question of "rights," and soon found myself adding the adjective "natural." The hide-bound realists, with whom, up to this point, I counted myself, reject the doctrine of natural rights as untenable; but their scoffing does not prove their case. While they explain "rights" as political delimitations of human behavior, they leave unexplained the justification or the political power to dispense "rights"—unless, indeed, the only justification for power is power, which is chaos again. If they adhere to the democratic theory, that "rights" inhere in the individual and that for practical purposes he lends them to his government, they must explain how the individual came by his "rights" in the first place. The realist's fear of the imagination leaves him without intellectual rudder.

Thus was undermined my faith in the inutility of faith. Putting aside organized religion, discounting ritual, rejecting theological doctrine, there still remained the necessity of establishing an unprovable "nature of things" as the final recourse of inquiry. Not that the "nature of things" offers an explanation for anything; but that the human mind must establish it as the compendium of those invariable forces which, when understood, help us to explain experience. The exigencies of life require that we go on looking to nature for its secrets, and maintaining faith that in them lies immutable law. And that, I believe, is the essence of the God-idea.

And "Natural Law"?

Thirty some years ago students of Henry George foresaw the coming of the New Deal, or something like it. The foresight stemmed from his chapter entitled "How Modern Civilization May Decline." In this he reasoned that the tendency of the wage level, regardless of productive increases, toward the point of mere subsistence, would open the way for State interference in economic affairs. Frustration and ignorance would demand it, and the politician, bent on his own purposes, would come forth with fantastic promises. Since politics is incapable of raising wages, but can only impose interventions which lower the productive level from which wages come, the result must be deterioration. New and more impossible promises would supplant the discredited ones. To carry them out the politician would ask for additional powers, including, of course, new tax levies. Political liberty would be put on the counter and offered at the bargain price of a mess of pottage. The eventual outcome would be a dictatorship—he called it, in 1879, an "imperatorship"—completely dominating all things economic, as well as political and social.

Henry George maintained that this consequence is not an historic imperative. It is no more necessary for society to go through the wringer of collectivism than it is necessary for a man to step off a high roof and break his neck. In the latter case, the man takes the consequence of defying an immutable physical law; and when society, said George, defies immutable laws in the field of economics it will likewise come to a bad end. Like the classicists before him, George was a firm advocate of natural law in economics.

It is not germane to this story to go into the economic theories of Henry George. What I had to encompass, and what I think is the basic economic issue of the present, is the doctrine of natural law. Briefly, this is the doctrine: nature has its own ways of applying means to ends, which are made known to us by critical observation; we observe in nature the constant recurrence of certain sequences, and because of that constancy we ascribe to the sequences a cause-and-effect relationship; we describe this presumably causal relationship in words or symbols, which we call natural law. The function of the "law" is to help us predict, to apply nature's means to our ends. Thus, when we observed that water always seeks its own level—a natural law—we were able to place our plumbing so as to bring about desired results.

Now, it is a certainty that nature does not ring a bell when we have hit upon one of her laws, and it is also a certainty that we have "discovered" some that subsequent investigation has shown up to be frauds. For these reasons the pragmatists reject the doctrine of natural law out of hand; there ain't no such animal, they say. They describe the constant sequences as probabilities; what has always happened, as far as we know, will probably recur in the future, but there is no assurance that it will. Natural law is a figment of the imagination, and so is causality.

Between the pragmatist and the transcendentalist there will never be more than a truce. Each represents a subjective attitude so deep-rooted that no objective meeting ground is possible. I believe I took to the natural law doctrine because of an inherent distrust of leadership; omniscience was too much to expect of the human and his integrity was equally questionable. I knew what faith in their wisdom has done to the priest and the politician, and students could be led astray if they took their professors to heart. Even in my college days I had fought it out with the socialists, before I knew the economic answers, on the ground that man's management of man is presumptuous and fraught with danger. I would rely on something less frail, something free of foibles, something impersonal. That something could be nothing else than nature. True, she is a rather elusive one, difficult to describe, let alone to handle, and philosophy could argue her non-existence. Nevertheless, she had proven herself a helpful fiction, if that is her real character, in the progress of mankind. I would trust her more than any man I ever knew or read about.

The difficulty, however, was that acceptance of the natural law doctrine called for faith in an order of things outside man and his works; and faith and I had been on the outs since I first laid all social difficulties at the door of religion. I had fortified myself against the God-idea implied in the natural law doctrine. In my study of philosophy I met transcendentalism with a knowing smile. Youth admits of no unconquerable ramparts of thought and attacks every unknown with complete confidence in its offensive powers. That is the proper function of youth, for from the vigor of its self-assurance our fund of knowledge does profit. But, when maturity comes to check up on youth's achievements the sum-total looks too much like spit and polish. The basic enigmas which youth inherits it passes on.

And so, I came to the God-idea because my rejection of it put rational thinking on a merry-go-round; there was no way of measuring the validity of an idea except by itself. The emotional storm which anti-semitism had stirred up caused me to throw overboard the anchor of reason. I had confused the organization which presumed to monopolize religion with religion itself, which is merely faith in the possiblity of an explanatory pattern of constancies. If nature cannot provide any guide to orderly thinking, any rules for an over-all harmony, then man's eternal search for one is silly. Must we look to parliaments for guidance? We might as well resign ourselves to wandering about in a maze of contradictions and quit trying to make sense of experience.

So, What Is a Jew?

When I was convinced that the primary cause of social discord is economic, I gave thought again to the so-called Jewish problem. Admitting, I said to myself, and to those who cared to listen, that some people delight in disliking Jews or any other minority, the matter would not come to violent hatred if everybody was always fully occupied at making a living and enjoying life. There would be no time for that sort of thing. And if it were realized that under proper conditions every pair of hands, even Jewish, add to the general fund of wealth, the dislike might be replaced by a healthier emotion.

Ofttimes, however, the getting of a living under our socio-economic arrangement is attended with frightening difficulty. At all times, except when war or its anticipation keeps us busy, there seem to be more willing to work than our economy can employ, and the competition for jobs is disheartening; not only are some forced to go without but those who are employed get relatively little out of it. This is bad enough in itself, but it looms still worse when the evidence of existing plenty is all too strong. To the discomfort of going without and the exasperation of futility is added a feeling of injustice; the unfairness is more maddening than the lack.

At this point in human affairs the pagan custom of locating a culprit comes upon us. Divinity is not immune from this habit of mind, for it is proclaimed, and proven with figures, that there are more mouths than nature can provide for, regardless of the pair of hands which accompany each mouth. The surplus population must be got rid of, one way or another. That's the answer of the pragmatic literate, who goes on to say that nature's way of balancing accounts is some form of mass slaughter. To the unlettered unemployed, however, a more specific culprit is necessary. Who took my job, who robbed me of my trade and my business? Peculiarly enough, the blame is always put on somebody who is least capable of defending himself from the charge or from any action that might be taken. In Texas it may be the Mexican; in California all economic troubles came from Oriental competitors; in New England, after the Civil War and even into this century, it was the Irish. The ex-slave has been an especially easy target, and then, of course, there is the Jew. There must be a culprit, as every reformer knows; would socialism have come as far as it has without the help of bosses, capitalists, bourgeois and fascists?

It is a very ancient custom, this business of scapegoats. According to the record, the Philistines served the Israelites in that capacity, while all the troubles of the Roman plebeian came out of Carthage. The peculiarity of the Jew is that he has served as scapegoat number one for nearly twenty centuries throughout the predominantly Christian world. Other minorities have been picked on at times, but wherever the Jew has made his presence felt in numbers he has held the lead role with little competition. The pogrom has been standard procedure whenever economic difficulties burst into social disaffection. Admitting the evidence of history on this point, there still remains the question as to why the Jew has been so consistently singled out.

We cannot dislike a people until we are convinced that these people are essentially different from us. It is easy then to establish inferiority. Our military men found, for instance, that hatred of the Germans was difficult to arouse, simply because it was difficult to establish as essential difference between the New Yorker and the Berliner, and tortuous argument had to be resorted to; with the Japanese the problem was quite simple for anybody so different from us in appearance must be inferior to us in capacities, to say nothing of character. Similar rationalization supports the disabilities put upon Orientals, Mexicans and Negroes in this country. The Jew, however, makes things difficult by offering a minimum of physical differences from his tormentor; his particularism had to be established.

This problem of identification was made easy by the Jew. He made himself a "different" kind of person long years ago. He accumulated a culture in the ancient days and has carried this culture, like necessary baggage, throughout his peregrinations. There is no doubt that where they have not suffered from segregation, or too confined segregation, Jews have added the culture of their neighbors to their own, sometimes to the point of self-submergence. Nevertheless, the indicia of their culture—which is the sum-total of those habits of language, tradition, religion, knowledge and mannerisms which an integrated people acquire—have left their mark. The mark becomes less visible as less notice is paid it, and more pronounced as persecution forces them back into themselves, for mutual protection and solace. It will be recalled that when Hitler began his anti-semitic campaign many a German Jew had to learn what it is to be a Jew; the culture was foreign to him.

One item in this culture needs to be emphasized at this time; I believe it is the one that has got the Jew into difficulties. That is the tendency toward self-expression which we call individualism. It may be that this characteristic stems from his ancient education (see the Hebrew Prophets), and it may be that it was brought on by necessity. At any rate, the Jewish child has drilled into him almost from birth the importance of self-improvement through self-help. Never is the individual taught that group excellence is more important than, or different from, individual excellence. It is he, the unit of the tribe, that makes it. Undoubtedly, this training shows up in an inordinate self-respect which, in a weak character, becomes irritating self-assertion. The point I wish to make is that Jewish culture is definitely not socialistic, even though tribal adherence has always been emphasized as a matter of self-preservation. That many Jews have advanced socialistic ideas is true, but I believe this can be explained as an inclination to protect against injustices, which is characteristic of the individualist. Karl Marx, it must be remembered, was an anti-statist, advocating the peculiar notion of abolishing the state through an interim dictatorship. Among the Old Bolsheviks were a number of Jews, more than their proportionate population would entitle them to; but it is significant that very few of them escaped the Stalinist purges; the Jew is too individualistic to be tolerated by the collectivism he sometimes urges.

Be that as it may, the differentiation which marks the Jew is cultural. A friend of mine, a scholar and agnostic, deplored the urge toward assimilation on the ground that the best in this culture would thereby be lost to mankind. However, it is his cultural idioms which identifies the Jew as a "different" sort of person, thus qualifying him for the role of minority scapegoat. Whether assimilation can completely eradicate these idioms is a question that cannot be decided until a long period of non-discrimination has permitted assimilation to take its course. So long as the institutions which bring about a scarcity economy are in force, the Jew will not divest himself of his historic role. The so-called Jewish problem, then—and this is true of all minority problems—is *at bottom* neither racial nor religious, but economic. Its eradication is dependent on the solution of the poverty-amidst-plenty problem. Maybe natural law can show the way; surely, the makeshifts of political law have failed.

CHAPTER 3

ABOUT
REVOLUTIONS

İT IS OBVIOUS that the world is knee-
deep in a social revolution. What is not obvious is that imbedded in the present revolution are the seeds of another.
Yet that must be so simply because it was always so. No
sooner do men settle down to a given set of ideas, a pattern of living and of thinking, than fault-finding begins, and
fault-finding is the tap-root of revolutions.

Many reasons are offered in explanation of this mental
restlessness. One reason that will serve as well as any other
is that we are born young, very young. It is the natural business of the young mind to ask "why," and since nobody has
answered that question with finality, the field for speculation is wide open. And so, as soon as youth finds flaws in the
going answers he makes up his own, and because they are

34

new, as far as he is concerned, they are guaranteed against flaw. Somehow the flaws do show up and another generation mounts its hobby horse in quest of the Holy Grail, the Brave New World. Revolution is inherent in the human make-up.

Suppose we came into this world with all the disabilities and disillusions of, say, the age of sixty. In that event, mankind would never have moved out of its cave apartments, never would have heard of the atom bomb or the New Deal. The only function of old men—or, at least, their only occupation—seems to be to find fault with the panaceas that possessed them in their youth. The price of experience is disillusionment. With disillusionment comes resistance to change, and the obstinacy goes so far as to find fallacies in the infallible panaceas of their sons. Nevertheless, youth hangs on to the ideas in which it has a proprietary interest, and change does come.

A revolution is a thought-pattern born of curiosity and nurtured on an ideal. Every generation thinks up its own thought-pattern, but because the preceding generation hangs on to what it is used to, the transition from the old to the new must be gradual. From the perspective of history it seems that on a certain date one revolution died and another was born. We think of the nineteenth century, with its tradition of natural rights, and its laissez-faire doctrine, as suddenly ushering in a reversal of the feudal tradition. But, Voltaire, Adam Smith, Rousseau and others were plowing and planting some time before 1800, and if you do some digging you'll find the roots of the nineteenth century in much earlier times. Even so, while we are enjoying, or rueing, our own revolution, it is a certainty that youth is critical of it and is building its successor.

There is a measure of fun, if you are inclined that way, in trying to discern in the prevailing current of ideas the direction of the next revolution. It is an interesting game, even if you know you cannot be on hand to say "I told you so." It is a game that takes the bitterness out of disillusion and robs pessimism of its gloom.

The Current Tradition

Our own revolution, the one that seems to have started on the first day of January, 1900, is identified by the doctrine of collectivism. Briefly, the doctrine holds that improvement in our way of living is attainable only if we discount the individual. The mass is all that matters. The doctrine does not deny the existence of the individual, but relegates him to the status of a means, not an end in himself. To support itself, the doctrine insists that the individual is only the product of his environment, which is the mass, that he could not exist outside of it, that he could not function except as an accessory to the mass.

The mass, on the other hand, is lacking in self-propelling force, and needs pushing. For this purpose a political machinery comes into existence, presumably by way of something called the democratic process. The individual serves the march of progress by submitting himself to the direction of that device. In the end, the doctrine holds, the individual will prosper because of the equal distribution of the abundance that comes from collective action.

That is the central idea of our current tradition. It is the idealization of the mass and the negation of the individual; its panacea, its method of realization, is political direction; its goal, as always, is the undefined Good Society.

So dominant is this doctrine in our thinking that it amounts to a dogma. It is implied, if not explicitly stated, in every field of thought. The aim of pedagogy today is not to prepare the individual for his own enjoyment of life, but to enable him to better serve the mass machine; the psychologist makes adjustment to mass-thought the measure of healthy thinking and living; jurisprudence puts social responsibility ahead of individual responsibility; the concern of the scientist in the discovery of principles is secondary to his preoccupation with mass production; the economist studies institutions, not people; and philosophy rejects speculation as to the nature of man or the purpose of life as effort that might better be put to the practical problems of society. Ours is the culture of "the all," rather than "the one."

The end-result of this kind of thinking, the practical result, is the worship of the State. This is a necessary consequence of the idealization of the mass, for since the mass can operate only under political power, then that power becomes the necessary condition of all life. It is a self-sufficient agency. It operates on a plane higher not only than that of the individual but also higher than that of the mass. It is not only super-personal, it is super-mass. Without the State the mass could not function, even if it could exist. The State, then, is the modern golden calf, with this essential difference, that its power is demonstrable, not assumed; it can and does guide, direct and harbor all of us. Hence, we adore it, make sacrifices to it and never question its infallibility, even if we detect inperfections in its hierarchy. The current president may be in error, but the State can do no wrong.

Our Fathers' Tradition

Just how far our revolution has gone along this path is seen when we make comparison with that of the nineteenth century. The dominant doctrine of that era held the individual to be the be-all and end-all of all life. He was the only reality. Society was not a thing in itself, but was merely an agglomeration of individuals working cooperatively for their mutual betterment; it cannot be greater than the sum of its parts. The individual was not the product of his environment, but the responsible master of it.

The nineteenth century had a dogma, too, and it went by the name of "unalienable rights." These were held to be personal prerogatives, inhering in the individual by virtue of his existence and traceable to God alone. Government had nothing to do with rights except to see that individuals did not transgress them; and that was the only reason for government. Its functions were entirely negative, like a watchman's, and when it presumed to act positively it was not minding its business; it must be called to account.

In the practical affairs of life, doctrines and dogmas have a way of losing their virtues; even integrated philosophies fall apart when men start applying them. The individualism of the nineteenth century suffered considerable mayhem, even from those who paid it most homage—the advocates of laissez-faire. Their insistence on their right to do as they pleased turned out to be the right to exploit others, a right they could not exercise without the help of the very State which they were pledged to hold in leash. They built up the power of the State by demanding privilege from it.

By the middle of the nineteenth century, this privilege-business had given individualism a bad character. The reality was far short of the earlier dream. Youth was quick to detect the fallacies in individualism as it was practised, condemned it and went to work on a replacement. The cure-all they hit upon was the doctrine of equalitarianism. Curiously, they promoted this new idea in the name of natural rights: if we are all endowed with equal quantity of natural rights then it follows that we all have an equal right to what everybody else has. That was, at bottom, not only a revolt against the injustices of privilege, but also a rationalization of covetousness. At any rate, equalitarianism called for an

extension of privilege, not the abolition of it; and since privilege is impossible without political enforcement, the equal-
itarians turned to State power for help. All kinds of reforms
were advocated, and all of them strengthened political
power at the expense of social power. It never occurred to
those who, like Dickens, struck a blow for bigger and better
"poor laws" that they were preparing the ground for social
security, which reduces the individual to wardship under
the State. Meanwhile, Karl Marx was developing his rationale for collectivism. The collectivistic revolution was born
in the matrix of individualism.

Revolutions Breed Revolutions

That is the point to keep in mind when we speculate on
the future, that revolutions are born in revolutions. And they
are always being born. Curious youth never fails to detect
inadequacies in the tradition it inherited and is impatient
to write a new formula. On paper, the formula is always perfect, and perhaps it would work out just as predicted if the
human hand did not touch it. Take the case of liberalism,
which was the political expression of the individualistic
thought-pattern. At the beginning of the last century, when
liberalism was emerging from adolescence, its only tenet
was that political intervention in the affairs of men is bad.
It traced all the disabilities that men suffered from to the
power of the State. Hence, it advocated the whittling away
of that power, without reserve, and proposed to abolish laws,
without replacement. This negativeness was all right until
the liberals got into places of power, and then it occurred to
them that a little positive action might be good; they discovered that only the laws enacted by non-liberals were
bad. The fact is—and this is something the State worshippers are prone to overlook—that the comforts, emoluments
and adulation that go with political office have great influ-

ence on political policy; for the State consists of men, and men are, unfortunately, always human. And so, liberalism mutated into its exact opposite by the end of the nineteenth century. Today it is the synonym of Statism.

Who knows what revolutionary ideas youth is toying with right now? We live entirely too close to the present to judge the direction of its currents. We are either pessimists or optimists, and in either case are poor witnesses. Those of us who are enamored of "the good old times" point to the prevalence of socialistic doctrine, particularly in class rooms and text books, as evidence that the "world is going to hell," while the proponents of socialism take the same evidence as proof of the immediacy of their millennium. Both sides are probably in error. It should be remembered that the present crop of teachers, who are also the text book writers, are the product of the socialistic tradition built up during the early part of the century, and are necessarily convinced of its virtue. Their denial of natural rights, for instance, is as natural as was the espousal of that doctrine by the teachers of 1850. However, the pessimists can take comfort in this fact, that though the professors do exert some influence on their students, they cannot stop curiosity. If the history of ideas is any guide as to the future, we can be sure that a change is in the making, that youth is brewing a revolution; it has been at the job throughout the ages.

To predict with any accuracy the tradition of the twenty-first century would require the equipment of a prophet. But, and here again relying on the evidence of history, we are on safe ground in anticipating a renaissance of individualism. For, the pendulum of socio-political thought has swung to and fro over the same arc since men began to live in association, and there is no warrant for believing that it will fly off in a new direction. Modern absolutism—going by the various names of communism, fascism, nazism or the less frightening "controlled economy"—is in many superficials quite different from "the divine right of kings"; but in their common rejection of the individual the two frames of thought are alike. Or, the individualistic doctrine of salvation that tarnished the glory of Rome had none of the economic overtones of nineteenth century individualism; but, the underlying idea of salvation is the primacy of the individual, not the collectivity, and that is the underlying idea of any form of individualism. A discarded tradition never returns in its former garb; in fact, it takes a lot of disrobing to recognize it. Only a historical expert can trace the New Deal of Modern America to the New Deal of Ancient Rome, or recognize Sparta in Moscow.

The Inevitable Future

Whatever the character of the coming revolution, it will not show itself until the present revolution has run its course. There is some disposition to try to stop it in its tracks, but that is in the nature of things a futile occupation. Even the opposition to the present collectivistic trend is tainted with it, as it must be. Those who fight socialized medicine tooth and nail would fight equally hard against a proposal to drop socialized education, unable to see that both institutions are cut from the same cloth; and those who view with alarm the teaching of collectivistic doctrine in our public school are simply plugging for a politically managed curriculum more to their own liking. Likewise, the "free enterprisers" rail against the subvention of farmers but are strong for the subvention of manufacturers through protective tariffs. We are immersed in prevailing tradition, and until it wears itself out and is replaced by another, nothing can be done about it. The best we can do is to find fault, which is the necessary preliminary to the coming revolution.

Of this, however, we can be sure: enrolled in some nursery

or freshman class right now is a Voltaire, an Adam Smith, a
Locke or a Godwin, some maverick who will emerge from
the herd and lead it. Youth, as always, is in a ferment, is
dissatisfied with things as are. Well, since the only direction youth can go is away from the current collectivistic
tradition toward its opposite, those who cherish the individualistic stock of values must try to peddle them to these
embryonic revolutionists. We must polish up our ancient
arguments, apply them to the current scene and offer them
as brand new merchandise. We must do a selling job. Youth
will not buy us out, lock, stock and barrel, but will be rather
selective about it; they will take what seems good to them,
modernize it, build it into a panacea and start a revolution.
God bless them.

CHAPTER 4

RETURN

REVOLUTION

IT ALL BEGAN, as you know, with the Declaration of Independence. The Americans stated their case, both as to the disabilities put upon them by the British Crown and as to the kind of government they considered it fitting for men to live under. The indictment was rejected and the issue was joined in battle. The god of war decided in favor of the Americans, insofar as removing the grievous rule was concerned; but in the establishment of a government to their liking the victors were on their own. Nobody could help them. Even history could not make a suggestion; for never had there been a political establishment constructed or operating on principles laid down in the Declaration.

These principles, moreover, were quite metaphysical,

completely outside the realm of experience. They were: one, that all men are created equal, and, two, that all men are endowed with inalienable rights. When you come down to it, the two metaphysical concepts are really one. For the postulate of equality did not apply to human capacities or attributes, which are quite unequal and far beyond the scope of government, but to the enjoyment of rights or prerogatives. In that respect, they maintained, all men must be considered on a par.

This was a brand-new base for government. In all political science hitherto known it had been an axiom that rights were privileges handed down to subjects by the sovereign power; hence there was nothing positive about them. A new king or a new parliament could abrogate existing rights or extend them to other groups or establish new favorites. The Americans, however, insisted that in the nature of things all rights inhere in the individual, by virtue of his existence, and that he instituted government for the sole purpose of preventing one citizen from violating the rights of another. Sovereign power, they said, resides in the individual; the government is only an agency of his will. If it fails to carry out its duties properly, or if it itself presumes to invade his rights, then the moral thing to do is to kick it out.

But, government is not an abstraction; it consists of people, and the inclination of all people is to improve upon their circumstances with whatever skills or capacities they possess and by whatever opportunities they meet up with. The power placed in the hands of this agency—to enforce the observance of an equality of rights—is in itself a temptation from which only the saintly are delivered. The Founding Fathers were therefore confronted with a difficult contradiction: men being what they are, a government is necessary; and government being what it is, men must be safeguarded against it. Their recipe was the Constitution. Whether or not the ensuing government would materialize the metaphysics of the Declaration, the Constitution was, at any rate, a definite pattern; and when it was ratified and put into operation, it became the end-product of the Revolution.

To be sure, the Constitution cut corners around the doctrine of natural rights. We must remember that it was, after all, a political instrument, concocted by men. Only in its preamble can such an instrument serve the moralities; its working parts must be geared to the interests of the dominating groups in society, and hence it must be a compromise; to effect the compromise the moralities must be watered down. The Constitution was no exception. The assumed equality of rights was distinctly out of line with the profitable slave-trade; owners of large estates wondered how it might affect their business; merchants and manufacturers deemed it dangerous to their preferred position. The Constitution was therefore so framed that the doctrine could not be employed to disrupt the status. There were many Americans who contended that the profit of the Revolution was liquidated by the Constitution and at their insistence a Bill of Rights was included.

The Basic Social Struggle

The Founding Fathers forged well. Putting aside what it might have been, the Constitution did pay homage to the doctrine of natural rights. It did so by the simple expedient of putting restraints and limitations on the powers of government. We learn from their published statements that the intent of the Founding Fathers was to prevent the despised "democrats," should they come into power, from using it for spoliation. They were quite forthright about it, and not a little could be said in favor of their thesis. In recent years the "mob" they feared has indeed come into

power and the result seems to support the contention of
Madison, Adams and Hamilton. But regardless of their argument and regardless of their intent, the Constitutional
shackles did in fact, though perhaps inadvertently, protect
the people in the enjoyment of their cherished rights.

From this we learn a little heeded lesson in social science,
namely, that the real struggle that disturbs the enjoyment
of life is not between economic classes but between Society
as a whole and the political power which imposes itself on
Society. The class-struggle theory is a blind alley. True,
people of like economic interests will gang up for the purpose of taking advantage of others. But within these classes
there is as much rivalry as there is between the classes.
When, however, you examine the advantage which one class
obtains over another you find that the basis of it is political
power. It is impossible for one person to exploit another,
for one class to exploit another, without the aid of law and
the force to back up the law. Examine any monopoly and you
will find it resting on the State. So that the economic and
social injustices we complain of are not due to economic
inequalities, but to the political means that bring about these
inequalities. If peace is to be brought into the social order it
is not by accentuating a class-struggle, but by restraining
the basic cause of it; that is, the political power. To bring
about a condition of equal rights, which is a condition of justice, the hands of the politician must be so tied that he cannot extend his activities beyond the simple duty of protect-
ing life and property, his only competence.

To the extent, then, that the Founding Fathers delimited
the powers of the new government—by the system of checks-
and-balances—to that extent did they render inestimable
social service. And to that extent did they insure the victory
of the Revolution.

The Three Immunities

For about a century and a half the American citizen enjoyed, in the main, three immunities against the State: in
respect to his property; in respect to his person; in respect
to his thought and expression. Pressure upon them was
constant, for in the pursuit of power the State is relentless,
but the dikes of the Constitution held firm and so did the
immunities. Only within our time did the State effect a vital
breach in the Constitution, and in short order the American,
no matter what his classification, was reduced to the status
of subject, as he was before 1776. His citizenship shrivelled
up when the Sixteenth Amendment replaced the Declaration
of Independence.

The income tax completely destroys the immunity of property. It flatly declares a prior right of the State to all things
produced. What it permits the individual to retain is a concession to expediency, not by any means a right; for the
State retains the liberty to set rates and to fix exemptions
from year to year, as its convenience dictates. Thus, the
sacred right of private property is violated, and the fact that
it is done *pro forma* makes the violation no less real than
when it is done arbitrarily by an autocrat. The blanks we so
dutifully fill out simply accentuate our degradation to
subject-status.

Demagoguery loves to emphasize a distinction between
human rights and property rights. The distinction is without
validity and only serves to arouse envy. The right to own is
the mark of a free man. The slave is a slave simply because
he is denied that right. And because the free man is secure
in the possession and enjoyment of what he produces, and
the slave is not, the spur to production is in one and not in
the other. Men produce to satisfy their desires and if their

gratifications are curbed they cease to produce beyond the point of limitation; on the other hand the only limit to their aspirations is the freedom to enjoy the fruits of their labors. That fact, deep-rooted in the nature of man, accounts for the progress of civilization when and where the right of property is recognized, and for the retrogression that follows from its denial. Property rights and human rights are more than complementary; they are identical.

The income tax did more than revoke the immunity of property. It gave the State the means of effectively attacking the immunities of mind and of person; it transferred to the State that sovereignty which, according to the American theory, is lodged in the individual. In the final analysis, sovereignty is a matter of dollars. The more dollars the more sovereignty. The individual is no longer sovereign when his living is dependent on a superior will, when that will becomes dominant by the economic strength behind it. The edicts of the State are not self-enforcing, since they lack the voluntary support of public opinion, and are therefore only as effective as the size of the police force; but the police force must be paid, and since the payments must come out of the property of those upon whom the edicts fall, there is no standing up to it. Without an F.B.I., military conscription —which violates the immunity of person—would be impossible; it failed during the Civil War simply because Lincoln did not have the funds to support such an agency. The Espionage Act—which violated the immunity of mind—would have been but a piece of paper but for the thugs hired by the State to enforce it.

Bribing the Constitution

Further, the wealth acquired by the State at the expense of the producers enabled it to buy its way into sovereignty. The Founding Fathers put a check on the central power by

clearly delimiting its scope, specifying that all other prerogatives, named and unnamed, shall reside in the component and autonomous commonwealths. They knew from
experience what a far-away and self-sufficient authority
could do to human liberty, and sought to avoid that danger
by making local government the residuary of all unspecified
power; not that the local politician is different in kind from
the national politician, but that his proximity to the people
makes him more sensitive to their will.

However, with the advent of the income tax this safeguard lost all meaning, for from then on the local politician
was less and less under obligation to his constituents; on
the other hand, they fell under his obligation by his ability
to hand out gratuities derived from federal grants, for which
he gave up nothing but the dignity vested in him by the
Constitution. His political preferment is now largely a matter of dispensing federal patronage. The American no longer
regards his local government as anything more than an
agency of the State. Thus, the original federation—the
Union—has been superseded in fact by a single, centralized
power, and the citizen of the commonwealth has become a
subject of that power. The income tax alone made this possible, inevitable.

The transmutation of the Constitution by bribery has
also been effected through private channels. The income tax
has made the State the largest single buyer in the country
and, since "the customer is always right," it is unthinkable
that the recipients of its patronage would oppose the State
on any issue important to its purposes. Subvention of agriculture, education and the press has been supplemented by
gratuities to sundry pressure-groups, all easing the shift of
sovereignty from the individual to the State. To top it all off,
the capital absorbed by the State, via the income tax, has
put it into business in a big way, so that it is now the largest

employer in the nation; loyalty to a boss of that potential
breeds a peculiar kind of freedom of conscience.

Lost Will for Freedom

Our forefathers were not unaware of the inverse ratio of
taxation to liberty. Their experience with the British Crown
was still fresh when the Founding Fathers came up with
the Constitution, and they scrutinized its taxing provisions
most carefully. About the only fiscal power generally conceded to the federal authority was a levy on imports. Hamilton knew this would hardly yield enough to support the
establishment contemplated and pleaded with great acumen
for the right to levy internal excise taxes. His argument pre-
vailed, but only because, as he pointed out, without this
revenue the government would be compelled to ask for the
unthinkable: a land tax or an income tax. And, until 1913,
the federal establishment had to get along as best it could
with what it picked up from custom duties and a few excise
taxes. Its sovereignty was thus contained.

In 1913 the relationship between the State and Society
was reversed. Areas which had heretofore been considered
within the private domain, sacred ground so to speak, were
now invaded by the arrogant and enriched State, and within
thirty years the individual was squeezed into a corner so
small that even his soul lacked elbow-room. His case was far
worse than it was in 1776; in exchange for an income tax
King George III would have conceded every point made
against him by the colonists, and might even have done
penance for past sins. But, such was the character of these
Americans that they challenged him to battle because he
presumed to impose a miserable tax on tea. What they won
at Yorktown was lost by their offspring one hundred and
thirty-two years later.

Were the disposition of the current crop of Americans

comparable to that of their forbears, a new revolution, to regain the profit of the first one, would be in order. There is far more justification for it now than there was in 1776. But, people do not do what reason dictates; they do what their disposition impels them to do. And the American disposition of the 1950s is flaccidly placid, obsequious and completely without a sense of freedom; it has been molded into that condition by the proceeds of the Sixteenth Amendment. We are Americans geographically, not in the tradition. In the circumstances, a return to the Constitutional immunities must wait for a miracle.

CHAPTER 5

THE NEED OF
A GOLDEN CALF

We HAVE it on the authority of the
Lord, as recorded in Genesis, that idolatry is a corruption far
more reprehensible than even the sins of the flesh. But, why?
Why is the inveterate habit of humans to worship idols put
so low in the scale of values? For answer, let's look to the
story of the golden calf.

It will be recalled that Moses had gone up to Sinai for
instructions on the management of his tribesmen, and because he had been gone so long about it they gave up on
him. So, they turned to Aaron, the second in command, and
demanded that he provide them with gods "which shall go
before us." That is, they wanted something tangible, sensual
and pragmatic to worship, the kind of gods they had seen in
Egypt.

A "Thick Cloud"

Moses had given them Jehovah, maintaining that He was the one and only. But this Jehovah, despite the fact that He had done quite well by them in their escape from bondage, turned out to be only an idea. He was intangible, unapproachable, completely out of this world and therefore difficult to comprehend. Even Moses saw Him only as a "thick cloud." When you get right down to it, Jehovah was an abstraction, and an abstraction is elusive; a graven image, like the dome on the capitol in Washington, can be seen and appreciated, and the worship of it is satisfying.

The most irritating thing about Jehovah was His insistence on principles. He would have no truck with expediency, was constantly bringing up long-run consequences, and scolded unmercifully when a fellow gave way to some momentary inclination of the flesh. He enjoined you to keep your eyes off the neighbor's wife and property, gave you no peace when you indulged your appetite for homicide, perjury or adultery.

This was most annoying. Other people had gods quite amenable to amendment; one could not only see and talk to them, one could do business with them. If only their palms were properly greased with sacrifices, they could be depended upon to produce anything you wanted, even social security, and no questions asked. Jehovah, on the other hand, was uncompromising. He laid down His inflexible principles, and you had to go it on your own from there. The best He could offer you was an opportunity—the Promised Land—and if you didn't have sense enough to make use of that opportunity you took the consequences. There was no way of getting around this intractible Jehovah.

Like all the people who came before or after them, the Jews found these undemonstrable absolutes rather confining. They resented having their aspirations restricted by the

natural order of things, their appetites delimited by industry and thrift. They wanted a handout, and on a golden
platter. That's what gods are for, and if Jehovah could not
or would not deliver on demand, they would set up reasonable gods. Hence, when Moses took an unconscionable time
in getting back from Sinai, and they thought they were
through with him and Jehovah for good and all, they went
pragmatic. They put in an order for gods capable of producing an inexhaustible supply of bread and circuses.

Aaron had no mind to argue with them. Though he is
listed in the Bible as a priest, the evidence shows him to have
been something of a politician. For one thing, the Lord assigned him to Moses as a spokesman, or rabble-rouser, when
the latter pleaded his lack of eloquence as a disqualification
for leadership. Aaron was selected because he was not "of a
slow tongue." Better proof of his political gift is the way he
handled the clamor for the golden calf: he heeded the will
of the mob, as a good leader should, and then he taxed them
so that he could give them what they wanted. And it was a
stiff tax, in those days: "Break off the golden earrings which
are in the ears of your wives, and of your sons and daughters,
and bring them to me."

Political Expediency for Natural Law

Having produced, out of their substance, the idol of their
hearts, Aaron followed the political pattern by declaring a
day of thanksgiving: "Tomorrow is a feast to the Lord."
(Notice, he wasn't breaking with tradition by denying the
Lord, but was insinuating divine sanction for the molten image; just as latter day Aarons are wont to equate democracy
with planning.) And the people had bread and circuses,
even as in the days of the Caesars and the New Deal. Everything was on a practical and immediate basis, with no
thought of consequences. Principles were abolished.

But, were they? Moses had insisted that principles were oblivious of human dicta, that they scoffed at abolitionists and went on operating in their accustomed way. If people presumed to conduct their affairs without regard to principles, they would suffer the consequences. And so, the principles that Aaron arrogantly disregarded continued to plague the Jews. According to the record, Jehovah waxed wroth with these backsliders and determined to wipe out the lot of them. Though we are told that Moses, with a marvelous piece of special pleading, dissuaded the Lord from His fell purpose, the fact is that civil war broke out among the Jews: "and there fell of the people that day about three thousand men."

In modern terminology, we would say that when you substitute political expediency for natural law (which is what idolatry amounts to), you are in for trouble: civilization becomes decadent and declines. The Bible puts it more dramatically: Moses got real sore, broke up the tablets on which the principles were inscribed, and all hell broke loose.

How long this condition continued is not clear, for the Bible is a bit careless about chronology. Judging by what we know about the decline of civilizations, it is a reasonable inference that a number of generations must have come and gone before the Jews recovered from their defiance of fundamental principle; in the Biblical story the whole transition seems to have happened within a few days. At any rate, after the Lord had decimated the tribes, and Moses had put the remnants back on the right track, there was what we call a rebirth of civilization. Or, Moses went up to Sinai, got a new set of tablets, and led his people to the Promised Land.

Like the Jews in the Wilderness

No one, and least of all those who are concerned with reform, will maintain that the human race has as yet reached the Promised Land. The evidence is all against it. Man has done a lot in accumulating a knowledge of things in general, but he seems incapable of ridding himself of the need of a golden calf. He still yearns for "gods which will go before us," gods that are uninhibited by the laws of nature, gods that are accountable only to our appetites, gods that speak not of consequences or the long run. In that respect we are like the Jews in the wilderness. Witness the pervasive religion of our times, the worship of the State.

Is not the State an idol? Is it not like any graven image into which men have read supernatural powers and super-human capacities? The State can feed us when we are hungry, heal us when we are ill; it can raise wages and lower prices, even at the same time; it can educate our children without cost; it can provide us against the contingencies of old age and amuse us when we are bored; it can give us electricity by passing laws and improve the game of baseball by regulation. What cannot the State do for us if only we have faith in it?

And we have faith. No creed in the history of the world ever captured the hearts and minds of men as has the modern creed of Statism. Men may differ in their rituals, they may call themselves Americans, Englishmen or Russians (New Dealers, Socialists or Communists), but in their adherence to the doctrine of the omnipotence of the State they are as one. It is the universal religion. There may be some who maintain the State is a false god, that it is powerless in the face of natural law, incapable of doing anything the individual cannot do for himself, and is in fact a hindrance to man in his effort toward self-improvement; but such dissidents from the norm are few indeed. From New York to Moscow to Peiping, and all way stations between, men pay homage to the State. It is a universal passion equal in intensity, but much larger in scope, to the spirit of the Crusades.

In the Moslem world, men turn toward Mecca at certain times of the day and pray to Allah according to prescribed rules. In America, all hands are constantly outstretched toward Washington, shamelessly demanding alms, subventions and whatever else their hearts desire, accompanying their prayers with threats of retribution if their supplications be denied. The din of the litany of "gimme" is heard all over the land. School teacher and banker, war veteran and labor union aristocrat, business man and college president, cry out in unison: "Thou who canst do all, do unto me more than thou dost unto others."

The Religion of Statism

And what is Washington but the shrine of the largest golden calf in the world? Here men of all degree come to press their claims on the provider of all things good. Here dwell in splendor the high priests of the church, and those upon whom the graven image grins favorably, while those who have not yet attracted its attention fan their hopes. There is no other occupation in Washington than to propitiate the god of gods. Throughout the day, in its many-tiered houses of worship, splendid in construction and air-conditioned for comfort, high-heeled cattlemen from Texas and high-hatted tycoons from Wall Street vie with one another in obeisances and genuflections; and in the evening, worn out by their devotions, the worshippers foregather at cocktail parties to repair their energies for tomorrow's prayers.

As for the substance of this religion of Statism, the absolute upon which its theology is based, it is that political power can do anything. There is no limitation upon its scope, except a contrary and more potent political power. Of a cer-

tainty, say its theologians, there are no "natural laws" to
hamstring the State; that is a well-exploded myth of the dark
ages. We have seen, they declare, how through the use of
force every so-called immutable consequential relationship
has been made mutable and inconsequential. All things are
relative. There are no certainties, either in the nature of man
or the nature of the world. In fact, there is no nature. Whatever men set their hearts on doing that will be done, provided only that they put their collective powers to the job.
And whatever the collective powers of men accomplish, that
is "good," simply because it "works." The religion of Statism
is thoroughly pragmatic; sufficient unto the day is the ac-
complishment thereof.

The State is the true god, its votaries maintain, because
it is immortal. Men come and go, the State lives on. The
priesthood who tend it may be Republicans or Democrats or
what-not; the State outlasts them all. It is self-sufficient because it is sovereign, omniscient because it has an intelligence superior to the combined intelligence of all men, beyond censure because its morality transcends that by which
mere man lives. It is not a social contract, not the product of
a body of laws which men make and unmake. It can say, as
the God of the Bible said of Himself—"I Am."

Yet, the State does not say that, or anything else, for it is
in fact only a golden calf. We who worship the fiction endow
it with superhuman gifts and capacities by merely demanding of it accomplishments that presuppose such gifts and
capacities. It is good because we want it to be. Out of the
fervency of our prayers comes the State.

Were we to take the trouble to examine the product of our
imagination, we would find the State to be only a body of
men who, taking advantage of our weakness, make the best
of it. They promise; because of our self-deception, we do not
question their ability to make good; nor do we take notice of

the contingent clause accompanying the promise, that we give them power over our persons and our property. Because they are human, because they, too, are incapable of defying or circumventing the laws of nature, they cannot do for us what we cannot do for ourselves, and their promise is never fulfilled; but, the power they have acquired is not relinquished. Thus, the State consists of a body of men who, by virtue of our need for a golden calf, acquire the power to compel us to do what we do not want to do.

In the present circumstances, seeing how far we have gone in the worship of the State, we are probably in for a smash-up similar to that which befell the Jews when they asked Aaron for "gods which shall go before us." We could use a Moses to put us on the track of first principles.

CHAPTER 6

IN DEFENSE OF
THIEVES

WALL STREET—which is a thorough-
fare completely surrounded by rumor—has a new tidbit on
its whispering tape. It is told in confidence, guaranteed "in-
side dope," and therefore is of doubtful character. Nevertheless, it is worth repeating.

The Department of Justice, the story goes, is hard after an
important corporation with a restraint-of-trade suit. This
juridical farce, which never gets to the bottom cause of monopoly, is an expensive nuisance that the company would
like to avoid; expense is of no moment to the department.
During the present sparring stage, something akin to blackmail enlivens the story. Certain people, credited with "having the ear of the White House," have approached the corporation with a bargain offer, to wit: the investigation will

be called off if the corporation will agree to load its executive payroll with a few friends of the Administration.

The significance of this story, regardless of its factual content, is that it is being told and believed. Forty years ago it would have been laughed at; it would never have been thought up. For, in those days it was taken for granted that the politician was a menial in the employ of Big Business. The idea that the hireling could "put the heat on" the men who made him would have been unthinkable.

The incidence of power has changed, and that is the point of the Wall Street rumor. When you read Gustavus Myers's *History of the Great American Fortunes*, or Lincoln Steffens's account of the muckraking era, in his *Autobiography*, you learn how Big Business made presidents, bought legislators and dictated judicial decisions. Up to early in this century, according to these historians, the political machinery of this country was an adjunct of monopoly. If a franchise was wanted, or a grant of land or a lucrative contract, the thing to do was to pack the legislative or executive branches with men of the right kind of integrity. There might be a fight between one gang of privilege-hunters and another, between a Gould and a Vanderbilt, and the fight might reach the sacred legislative halls, but the respective agents of these men simply carried out orders; they rarely presumed to do otherwise. Their recompense was the security of political preferment, so long as they remained dutiful servants, with participation in the loot if they were particularly useful.

How times have changed! The rumored hold-up of a corporation by politicians may be apochryphal; but it is a fact these days that corporations frequently find it advantageous to man their executive positions with men whose sole recommendation is political background. A general who commanded a desk at the Pentagon is put in command of an airplane factory; a chief of police is made vice-president of a utility company; an ex-member of the presidential cabinet is hired to run a bottling works; the baseball business reaches into the Senate for a custodian of its affairs; the son of a president becomes overnight an expert in insurance. Why? Tradition once held that the man who could best run a business was one who had learned it from the bottom up. Now, it seems, such training is unnecessary; it is far more important that the head of a corporation know his way around in political circles. This qualification is so important that many a top executive is drawn to Washington for a finishing course.

This turn of events indicates that Big Business has lost its dominance over Politics. The bureaucrat is in the driver's seat. The successors of the robber barons of the nineteenth century operate on sufferance; the obsequiousness of their lobbyists in Washington is pitiful to behold. Is the change of leadership in the best interests of our economy?

Let's put aside any moral evaluation of the old time method. We can concede that the egregious railroad land-grants amounted to thievery; the right of the people to the use of this land was abrogated without any warrant in ethics, and the operations of the Hills and the Harrimans, in cahoots with servile legislators, were little more than a confidence game. Nevertheless, it cannot be denied that these men did build railroads. Their motive was profit, to be sure, even though they prated about building an American empire. But, production has to precede profit. They had to provide a transportation service. What they got from their elected servants was an exclusive privilege, enabling them to wangle a monopoly profit out of the users of the railroads, more than they could have got out of competitive business.

Furthermore, the miles and miles of land handed to them were useless until exploited. Purely for their own selfish interests the railroad barons induced farmers and artisans to settle on their ill-gotten lands. Commercial and industrial centers sprang up on the sites they had acquired from the "people's representatives," and through sales and rentals their fortunes prospered. They encouraged production, for only in that way could they cash in.

The Weyerhausers had to cut, transport and sell the lumber from the lands they had slyly come by, or all would have been in vain. The lumber would surely have been put to good use even if these lords of the forest had not managed themselves into titles; people use the gifts of nature not because they are owned but because they are necessary to the satisfaction of human desires. But, that is beside the point; the barons could not have cashed in on their legally-supported rackets unless they produced, or caused to have produced, the good things that are made of wood.

And so with the oil wells, the mines, the traction franchises, the choice city lots that the Astors and the Fields and the Trinity Corporations got title to by legal, though un-Christian means; in every case ownership paid off through use. Since production is synonymous with life, or is at least the measure of its material fullness, something can be said for the social usefulness of these anti-social monopolists. They worked society for all it was worth, but in so doing they inadvertently contributed something to society.

As for the public servants who served these robber barons, what else could they do? Despite the delusion of "clean politics," the only use to which political power can be put is the creation of privilege. Theoretically, government can be "good," but only if its functions are restricted to the protection of life and property; but, to that purely negative occupation rulers have never confined themselves, and there is some doubt that the ruled would be satisfied with that kind of government. In practice, the art of ruling settles down to the granting of economic privileges to a few, to the disadvantage of the many; the beneficiaries of these privileges are either the politicians themselves or their supporting patrons. Nothing can be done about eradicating this practice until "you and I" learn what privilege is and are willing to get along without it. Whether "you and I" are susceptible to that kind of education is a moot question.

However, the realistic plunderers of the nineteenth century were cognizant of the limited capacity of the political person and kept him in his place, which was the back room of a saloon. The innate puppet was allowed to flatter his ego in a peroration from the tail of a torch-lit wagon; and there he stopped. His training and his inclination being what it is, he never presumed to barge in on the management of the businesses he helped to create; he would have been thrown out if he had tried. He did all he was expected to do, or was capable of doing, when he voted "right."

The reformers would not let him be. For over a hundred years these disciples of heaven-on-earth-through-politics came at the poor politician with vitriolic castigation. They threw out one "rascal" after another, and seemed unable to get any other kind in power; somehow the shining armor of the glorious crusaders began to tarnish as soon as they entered the lists. Some reformers traced the continuity of rascality to a nebulous "system" and each came up with a formula that would most surely do away with this evil. Even though the formulae frequently contradicted one another, they all contained the same activating ingredient: More Political Power. This fact could hardly escape the politician forever; the reforms would most certainly improve his own position, whether they accomplished the advertised purpose or not. In his shrewd way he perceived that the reformers were after privileges for other groups than those he had been serving, and at privilege-making he was an expert.

So, the politician hopped to the reforms. He created new privileges right and left. The land-grabber, the right-of-way thief, the tariff vulture and the unscrupulous contractor were not neglected; it was not necessary, for nobody asked for the abolition of privilege; all wanted more. Farmers, veterans, unemployed—any substantial group that could "deliver the vote"—were invited to the festival. This abundance of free lunch had to come from somewhere, and where can the poor politician, the inherent non-producer, get it? From taxation, of course. He gave and he taxed. The ward-heeler was transformed into a bureaucrat by reforms.

We hear less and less about the "system" these days, and the enthusiasm for "clean" politics has given way to the worship of power. Liberality in the diffusion of privilege has raised the politician to the pinnacle of high-priest while the increase of taxation has made us more and more and more dependent upon his beneficence. From this consequence of reform it would appear that what we all want, regardless of the moralisms we spout, is something "for free." The robber barons whom the reformers lambasted during the nineteenth century did what each of us would do if endowed with his courage and presented with the opportunity, and the "crooked" politician is merely a reflection of ourselves. To put it another way, the politician is as "clean" as his constituents.

The diffusion of privilege in all directions had the marvellous result of freeing the politician from vassalage to any one gang. In the old days he might play one group against another, he might even take bribes from both; but, after he had befouled himself he was no longer a free agent; he was a tool. Long before 1933, such reforms as the direct election of senators and woman suffrage had weakened the hold that Big Business had upon him, and the prohibition movement showed him that even organized religion was amenable to

political reason. The New Deal, of course, completely liber-
ated him from his old dependency; for here was in one
package all the "social legislation" needed to build up a supporting cast of diverse interests. Now he could flaunt the
union crowd in the face of the haughty Union League; the
railroad magnates took a secondary place in his loyalty after
"parity" had won him the hearts of the farmers; reciprocal
trade treaties put in his hand a weapon against arrogant
protectionists; there was no "economic royalist" powerful
enough to stand up to the powers of intervention he had
acquired by reform.

To be exact, the unshackling of the politician began in
1913, when the Sixteenth Amendment handed him the economic key. After that, as exigencies permitted, he could buy
the loyalty of the jobless with sustenance, or the support of
entire sections by voting it gratuities supplied by other sections. This limitless income meant bigger contracts and more
liberal subsidies with which to buy the adulation of indus-
trialists, bankers and housewives. Now he could be the bribe-
giver, rather than the bribe-taker. The income tax completely
changed the character of the American politician.

Whether or not the reforms made him "clean," they certainly made the politician powerful. Every reform calls for a
law, and every law contains an enforcement clause; if the
law were self-enforcing it would not have been necessary.
Enforcement means a detail of police, which is the reality of
political power. But, the law cannot anticipate the scope of
human imagination, nor contain human cupidity, and it is
not long before a loophole in the law is discovered by ingenuity. Then comes a new law to plug up the loophole, which
invariably creates a new loophole, calling for another law.
And all of the laws demand enforcement agencies. Thus,
the practical result of all reforms is to inflate the importance
of the politician; first, as administrator of the law, and then

as a guide through the confusion caused by the multiplicity of laws. In this scheme of things, he becomes indispensable to Big Business, Big Education, Big Unionism, Big Anything. Enterprise of any kind cannot manage without him, and his services—at an honorarium, not a bribe—are sought for.

However, this "clean" politician cannot bring to the marketplace a single good, any more than his unwashed predecessor could. There is a widespread superstition that politics can in some way, and without any expenditure of effort on our part, feed, clothe, house and enrich all of us. It is this superstition that spawns all reform movements. Yet the incontrovertible fact of history is that politics is purely an expense, a drain on the marketplace, and cannot be anything else. When we add up the results of all the reforms that have come to fruition in this country, we see that the bottom figure comes to one-third of all "you and I" produce. It would be impossible for accountants to prove it, but casual observation suggests that the combined thievery of all the Morgans, Stanfords, Fisks *et al.*, which includes the bribes they paid to politicians, never came to fifty billions per annum. What price reform!

It has come to pass, then, that those who once danced to the fiddles of the Empire Builders now call the tunes. They wend their way into the management of industries for which they have no other competence than their knowledge of the loopholes in the constrictive laws they helped to enact. Their main qualification for executive position is their comradeship with those who administer the laws, and the only service they can render their employers is the complaisance which this comradeship can secure. The current jargon gives them the nice title of "public relations men." Since, however, they contribute nothing to the process of production, of adding to the abundance of the marketplace, the salaries of these political appendages to business must be put into the category of bribes. Just like bribes, their pay-checks show up in the prices the public must pay for the products. Or, like the "protection" paid to racketeers.

This dependence of industry on politics must continue; the politician will see to it, by passing new laws, and the industrialist, looking only to immediate profits, will encourage his own extinction. So long as the Sixteenth Amendment is in force, the industrialist must play a less and less important role. The next step? One needs hindsight, rather than the gift of prophecy, to foretell the demotion of the entrepreneur and the technician to still lower positions in the economy, and the ascendancy of the non-productive politician to top-control; it happened in Germany and Italy.

Well, if it must be it must be. But, one cannot put away a nostalgic throb for the old buccaneers. They were ruthless but bold; selfish in the grand manner; cunning gamblers who dealt from the bottom without blinking an eyelid; battlers who respected only the laws they made. And, they were builders. True, they plundered what they built, but despite the capacity of their maws, they did leave a capital structure behind. The economy of America was a bit richer for their having lived. For all their stealing, they gave us something that politics is incapable of matching.

Nor can one avoid a feeling of pity and disgust toward those who have taken over the throttle once held by these picturesque pirates. The new crop still think of themselves as captains of industry, but, like the top-sergeant before his commanding officer, they eat humble pie in the presence of a politician. What a raucous laugh must shake the halls of the Valhalla where dwell the souls of the nineteenth century thieves as they watch the steady procession of tin-cup bearing magnates from Wall Street to Washington. In their day the parade marched the other way.

When, as now seems inevitable, the American soul will

have been well inured to the coming serfdom, it is more than likely that the old gang will provide the material for a new romantic saga. The evil they wrought will have been interred with the muckrakers who exposed them, while the story of their daring self-assertion will serve as a vicarious fillip for the grovelling American of tomorrow. They will replace, in our story books, the sword-sticking illiterates of the glamorous eighteenth century, and the unbathed gun-toters of our Wild West. The generation in the offing will sublimate their repressions in the tales of these American scoundrels. Hollywood might look to the prospect now.

CHAPTER 7

OPEN LETTER

TO JOE

Dear Joe:

Everybody is writing you letters. Don't let this annoy you, for with us Americans writing letters to editors, congressmen and other celebrities is only a national habit. It's in line with what we call democracy—if you will pardon the expression.

Let me assure you that my presumption in addressing you stems from a sincere concern for the success of your program. I am not one of those who are bent on reforming you. Far from it. You are The Perfect State; to even suggest improvement is superarrogation. I suspect that the criticism hurled at you, particularly from our own neophytes in the business of Statism, springs from envy and is in fact only left-handed admiration. You are the Ideal of every Statist in the world, including the pip-squeak professors who try to show with calculus how you can be bettered, as well as the "democratic" boy scouts in Washington who hurl epithets at you. Don't let these amateurs bother you. You are tops!

Your mission is world conquest. Good! That has always been the goal of The Perfect State. Other fellows in the past have failed in the attempt, but that is no reason why you should fail. You have more than an even chance of making it. The only hurdle in your path is the Bungling State at Washington, and I want to tell you just how you can remove it. That's why I am writing you.

II

It seems to me your present course is hurting your chances. You are building up your opposition. By supplying the Bunglers with a scarecrow you are making it possible for them to build up a State here that would give you a run for your money. Chief Bungler Harry is not strong on knowledge and probably never heard of the Marxist maxim that the way to destroy private property (and thus establish a top-drawer State) is to tax it out of existence. Despite his lack of book learning, he is learning fast, principally because he has seen how you do it.

Harry's difficulty is the American tradition of private property, to which we still give lip service, and Harry can't break through this tradition without a permanent "dire emergency." You know how important it is for the State to work on the herd instinct and how necessary for that purpose is a first class bogeyman. Everything you have been doing these past five years has helped to build you up as the bogeyman supreme, and unless you change your tactics Harry will make use of you to confiscate every bit of property in the country, and then you will have a real State to contend with.

I have no illusions about your predatory ambitions. You've

got to have a war to stay in business and a successful war with this country would suit you fine. Your native slaves are undoubtedly kicking up a fuss over their rations; a diversionary war might be *comme il faut* in the circumstances. And you are undoubtedly thinking about the confusion and the ineffectiveness of our defense measures, and how much easier it would be for you to attack now and not wait until some sound program, like that proposed by Herbert Hoover, is put into effect; the aimless plans of Mr. Truman and Gen. Eisenhower might be more propitious for you.

However, the question is, is this the proper time to get going on your war? I don't think so. I believe I can show you that if you put off your war for a couple of years, despite internal difficulties, your prospects for success would be improved. If you will correct your timing, Joe, you should be able to achieve the first World State in history. You will achieve what a lot of fellows, from Ghengis Khan down to FDR, only dreamed about. Listen to my argument.

III

For some time now our economy has been geared to war. More and more we have been producing for waste, not consumption. Every machine in the country is turning out something that, directly or indirectly, contributes to the stockpile of destruction, and every worker is engaged in providing fodder for the management of that stockpile. We still talk of "business" as if it were the process of the production of goods and services, of things people want, but the fact of the matter is that for several decades more than a third of all our production has been going down the rat hole. (Look at the tax figures.) At this writing, due to the scare resulting from your poor timing, the proportion is increasing; within a year, the way things are going, at least half of our time will be put into feeding the State.

To drive home the point, our armed forces and our bureaucrats now total approximately six million non-producing consumers, and that comes to about ten per cent of our employable population. The other ninety per cent are thus "fully employed." I needn't tell you, an expert in these things, that besides being busy we are quite rich, thanks to the printing presses.

You know all this, but what you are apparently losing sight of is that all this "prosperity" rests on you. Without you as Bogeyman Number One all this busyness would be impossible. Our economy is so constructed that without an "enemy" it would collapse. Of course, the economics professors could undoubtedly frame another reason for continuing along these lines, but that would take some time. Right now the structure of American "business" is supported by none other than Joe Stalin, and his removal from the scene would be a calamity.

You should see what I am driving at. Some of your economists have been predicting the smashup of what remains of our capitalistic system these past five years, and have been advising you to wait for it before making your war-move. Report has it that because the smashup has not come you have put these boys in the doghouse. You must not be so hard on them. They simply did not take into consideration the support you yourself have given our economy; it even escaped your omniscience. Maybe if you had not supplied our neophyte Statists with plausibilities for spending ourselves into prosperity, things would be with us as your oracles predicted. You put off our "bust."

IV

Suppose you should pull the rug from under the boys who are managing our economy. You would leave them flat on their collective buttocks, and before they could pick themselves up—well, the thing you have been hoping for would happen. Without you to blame everything on, there would be no immediate excuse for spending billions on armaments, both for ourselves and our weak sisters in Europe.

What then? Our factories would shut down, millions would be out of work. There would be moaning and groaning all over the land. The proletariat would be joined by the capitalists in one general "relief" concert. Our "prosperity" would indeed be punctured.

So, the thing for you to do—and that is the purpose of this letter—is to remove yourself as the indispensable bogeyman. Pull a real peace offensive—right now. I don't mean one of those fake things you have been staging; these have obviously boomeranged in your face. I mean something that cannot be mistaken, say like marching your armies straight East out of Germany, and doing it without previous parliamentary palaver, without notice. You ought to be able to figure out some world-startling stunt that would leave our inept planners gasping for breath. The sudden realization that you cannot be counted on to support our economy would be most demoralizing.

What I am suggesting, if you think of it, is in line with what your immortal Lenin advised as sound Communistic strategy: one step backward and two steps forward. After you have upset our economic apple cart by the move suggested, and confusion is all over the country, you can then go ahead with your main purpose.

For, as you know, chaos always brings on a demand for a messiah. Some one will surely pop up. Whoever he is, he will be ideologically beholden to you, for there would be no better one to turn to. In fact, the logical candidate for the job would be one of the fellows you have planted in our bureaucracy, or in our unions, somebody who has been worshipping you all these years.

Permit me to nominate for the job somebody with a good old Anglo-Saxon name, maybe sporting a Phi Beta Kappa key. Or, you couldn't do better than to pick one of the ubiquitous Roosevelt clan.

There it is, Joe. Don't you realize now that an honest-to-goodness peace move right now is just what you need to get yourself a satellite across the Atlantic? Now, go to it.

Yours for the State Supreme,

FRANK

P.S. This advice is given gratuitously. If, however, you should think it of any value, and wish to recompense me, just put me wise about a week before you make your big move—but don't tell anybody else. I will notify my broker to place some "short selling" orders and, believe me, I will make plenty. And, about the time your armies start moving out of Germany I will take a walk down to the corner of Wall and Broad Streets to see what happens. I believe I will have to duck the bodies of the deflated millionaires as they drop from the tall buildings.

P.P.S. The newspapers are giving front-page space to the proposed Four Power Conference. It is reported that you had something to do with instigating this thing. In that case, it may be that you anticipated my advice. Good! However, let me warn you to watch our Washington boys. They talk a lot about peace, but I suspect they would like to keep the war-pot boiling. They don't want war, of course, but they certainly don't want peace—real peace—either. In order to keep in the saddle and to carry out their economic phantasmagoria they must have a permanent *delenda est Carthago;* in which capacity you have served well. So, be careful they do not maneuver you out of a real peace move at Paris.

CHAPTER 8

LET'S **TEACH** COMMUNISM

THIS IS a defense of our universities. As they open their doors for another year of business they labor under a wide-spread suspicion of teaching communism. The suspicion is unsupported by fact; it is pure witchcraft. There is reason to believe that some in the faculties *advocate* communism, but none *teach* it. The distinction is important. To illustrate the point, in the field of religion there are many who are intellectually incapable of comprehending Christianity, and therefore of teaching it, but who are quite adept at advocating (preaching) it. So with communism; it is a pattern of ideas following from basic assumptions, and unless one has made a critical examination of these assumptions one is incapable of evaluating the superimposed ideas. Our colleges are debarred from examining the basic assumptions of communism, because, as I will attempt to show, these basic assumptions are part and parcel of what is called capitalism, the going order, and it would hardly do to bring this fact to light.

If it is the business of universities to expose students to ideas, they are not doing the job properly if they neglect to include in their curricula a course in communism simply because as a system of thought, a philosophy, communism is in the ascendancy these days. A graduate ought to be thoroughly at home with the ideas he has to live with, he ought to understand the basic postulates of his ideological environment. It might be difficult to dig up professors able to brush aside the seductive phrases of communism so as to get to its roots, seeing how the subject is beclouded with war hysteria, and expedience might tell against the introduction of such a course of study. This is regrettable. For, lacking the opportunity to investigate communism, the students will come away from their education with the popular notion that it is indigenous to an "enemy" nation or an "inferior" people. To illustrate the kind of course I have in mind—this is *not* an application for a job; perish the thought!—I present herewith a few samples of communist theory that are equally the marrow of current "true Americanism." At random, we will begin with a conception of wages.

It is an axiom of communism that wages are a fraction of production given to the workers by those who own the means of production. Boiled down to its essence, this idea can be expressed in three words: capital pays wages. But, is that so in fact? If we define capital as the tools of production, this conception of wages becomes silly, for an inanimate object is incapable of paying anything. If, as the communists do, we include in the definition the owners of capital, we are faced with another *reductio ad absurdum:* competition between these machine-owners for the services of machine-users automatically fixes the level of wages; capitalists are without the means of affecting the ups and downs of that level.

The capitalist, of course, speaks of the wages he "pays." But, he is quick to point out that the wages do not come out of his capital, but are derived from the sale of his products; if the market does not absorb the output of his plant he ceases to be a "payer" of wages. This means that the envelopes he hands out to his employees are filled by the consumers, and these are, in large part, the workers themselves. Thus, the employer of labor is labor, and the wage-earner is the wage-payer. It follows that the general level of wages is determined by the general level of production—leaving out, for the moment, any purloining—and neither capital nor capitalist have any part in fixing it.

It follows also that political power can in no way affect an increase in wages; nor can capital by itself do so. Wages can go up only as a result of increased production, due to an increase in population or improvement in the skill and industry of the current population. That elemental fact will be admitted even by professors of economics, and it is possible that some legislators will recognize it. Yet, if you dig into some standard economics textbooks or examine the labor-legislation of our land you will find ideas that stem from the communist notion that capital pays wages and that the hard-hearted capitalist keeps them low. A minimum-wage law, for instance, is based on that notion; the law assumes that cupidity is at the bottom of the marginal worker's low income; the capitalists must be compelled to disgorge. All of which is silly, for the legally enforced increase is simply passed on to the consumer, unless it can be absorbed by increased production due to technological improvement. Yet, in the course I suggest, it would have to be pointed out that minimum wage laws—that all legislation dealing with labor-employer relations—are concessions to the communist conception of wages.

Our immigration restriction laws pay homage to this idea, for these laws, translated into economics, simply say that there are just so many jobs that capitalists have at their disposal, that any increase in the working population will lower the wage level by simple division; the idea that the immigrant makes his own wages is rejected off-hand. Birth control is likewise advocated as a means of raising the wage level, and Malthusianism borrows all its economics from communism. And, if you go to the bottom of our "social welfare" enthusiasm you will find the capital-culprit notion.

Space does not permit an examination of all the facets of current thought traceable to this basic bit of communism, but it is evident that the proposed course could do quite a job on it.

This brings us to the communist indictment of private capital. The inherent power of capital to fix the level of wages will be used by its owners to defraud the laborers. They will see to it that the laborers receive just enough to keep them alive and on the job, retaining all above that level for themselves. Here communism introduces the doctrine of natural rights, although it denies that doctrine vehemently later on; it says that the laborers have an absolute right in all that is produced by virtue of the energy put into production; energy is a private possession. If this is so, then what the capitalist keeps for himself amounts to robbery. The word generally used is "exploitation." This iniquitous arrangement brings on a host of evil social consequences and should, therefore, be stopped. How? By outlawing private capital. Everything that is produced should belong to the community as a whole (which, by the way, is a flat denial of the original right of the laborer to his product), and the State, acting for the community, must be made sole owner and operator of all capital. The State, particularly when manned by communists, will have no interest in exploitation and will pay wages in full.

The holes in that indictment are many and serious, and we can leave it to our professor in communism to point them out. It would then be incumbent on him to also point out that capitalism, in practice, accepts the indictment in large chunks. A number of institutions have grown up under capitalism that are obviously concessions to the charge brought against it by communism. The absorption by the State of large parts of the electric power business was facilitated by moral fustian about the "power trust," while political participation in the banking, housing, insurance and several other businesses is justified on the inadequacies, if not villainies, of private capital. Thus, while capitalism carries on its word-battle with communism it pays its adversary the high compliment of accepting its doctrine in practice.

Our professor of communism could, and should, emphasize this point by an analysis of taxation, particularly the direct kind. Income taxes unequivocally deny the principle of private property. Inherent in these levies is the postulate that the State has a prior lien on all the production of its subjects; what it does not take is merely a concession, not a right, and it reserves for itself the prerogative of altering the rates and the exemptions according to its requirements. It is a matter of fiat, not contract. If that is not communist principle, what is? The professor would have to point that out. And he should, in all conscience, show that the considerable amount of capital now owned and operated by the "capitalistic" State was siphoned out of pockets of producers by means of taxation.

But, right here the professor would find himself in a mess of trouble. On the other side of the hall the professor of taxation and the professor of political science would be telling their students that the right of property is conditional, not absolute, that the owner is in fact a trustee answerable to society as a whole. They would deny that this is a concession to communist principle, but it is. The professor of philosophy would pitch in with an outright rejection of the theory of natural rights, asserting that what we call rights are but privileges granted to his subjects by the sovereign. The board of trustees would also take notice; the university and its supporters hold a lot of government bonds which are dependent on the power of taxation, and it would hardly do to question the propriety of this power. And, if the professor presumed to point out that communism is quite consistent in advocating taxation as a means of destroying private capital, he would have the whole house of respectability on his head.

A few more topics that our course in fundamental economics should touch upon—and then we can close up shop.

Reverting to the concept of natural rights—basic in capitalistic thought—we find that its tap-root is the will to live. Out of this primordial desire for existence comes the idea that no man may lay claim to another man's life. How does that line up with military conscription? It doesn't, and the only way you can logically support conscription is to invoke the communist principle that the right to life is conditioned by the needs of the State.

Take the subject of monopoly. Communism makes much of it, although by a strange twist of logic it sees in State monopoly all the virtues lacking in private monopoly. Capitalism, in theory at least, equally condemns monopoly, on the ground that any restriction of competition lowers the general level of production and is a deterrent to human aspirations. An examination of the anatomy of monopoly reveals that its vital organ is the power to restrict production, and the source of this power is the State. Without some law favorable to its purpose every monopoly would disintegrate. Hence,

the very fact of monopolies under a regime of capitalism—
sometimes called "free enterprise"—lends support to the
communist assertion that the State is a committee managing
affairs for the benefit of monopolies.

In discussing monopolies the class would most certainly
hit upon the topic of exploitation; that is, any legal means
for getting something for nothing. Having disposed of the
untenable proposition that the ownership of capital is in itself a means of exploitation, the professor, being a man of
intellectual integrity, would be compelled to admit that the
object of monopoly is exploitation, and that the State, in
establishing the special privileges which spawn monopolies,
is the guilty one. He might go so far as to declare the State
—even the "dictatorship of the proletariat"—the only ex-
ploitative factor in any economy.

And so on and so on. In dissecting communism and expos-
ing its vital parts to view, this proposed course would
demonstrate the unpleasant truth that capitalist practice
too often squares with communist theory. That might prove
disquieting to the established departments of law, social
science, history—to say nothing of the mahogany office up
front. It might also disturb the students, inured as they are
to a quasi-communist quasi-capitalist environment.

Under the circumstances, no college could entertain the
idea of introducing into its curriculum a course in communism, and the charge that they are teaching the subject is
unfounded. That they make concessions to communist
theory in many of their courses is true, but that is a require-
ment put upon them by the as-is capitalism. And I might
add that I have no fear of being asked by any college president to offer the proposed course.

CHAPTER 9

THE TALE OF

TWO STUDENTS

THEY WERE members of the debating club at a local college, and would we please help them prepare for the debate:

Resolved, that the Federal Government should adopt a permanent program of wage and price control.

They had good reason for coming to us. HUMAN EVENTS had made editorial comment on this debate topic in a recent issue, and the students inferred that we were something of an authority. We are not immune to flattery, and the coed debater was pleasant to talk to.

To bring the matter up to date: Before the college season opens, some five hundred colleges submit to a central committee their ideas on what ought to be debated. The

committee consists of faculty representatives from four inter-
collegiate fraternities and a member of the American Society of Speech. These five sift the suggested subjects and
draft four resolutions that seem to embrace the major ideas.
The four resolutions are submitted to the member colleges;
the one receiving the highest vote becomes the debate of the
year.

Our editorial comment on the topic for 1951-1952 was that
it was "loaded"—the mere statement implies the acceptance
of a questionable premise. The premise is that a wage and
price control program is not only practical but even desirable;
that goes without saying, and the only matter left open for
discussion is the desirability of a permanent program. We
pointed out, also, that in the current textbooks, with which
we are familiar, the idea of controls is favorably treated, so
that the debaters on the negative side would be arguing
against what they had learned in class. If they debated well,
how would they fare in their economics examinations?

II

The notebooks were made ready. We adopted the Socratic
method. What is the purpose of price controls, we asked.

"To keep prices down, of course."

What made them high?

"A shortage of goods and a great demand."

Or an abundance of money, we volunteered. The controls
won't bring more goods to market and they are not intended
to reduce the amount of money in circulation. They simply
aim to compel sellers to accept, and buyers to quote, prices
lower than those prevailing in the free market.

"You are implying," said the young lady, "that there is an
immutable law of supply and demand. One of my books says
there is no such law."

Immutable, we ventured, is a long word leading to a long

argument. Would she be good enough to tell us what she would do, were she a dressmaker, if the fixed price of dresses were below her costs?

"I'd quit making dresses."

Unless she reluctantly accepted prices forced upon her by women who disregarded the law, we added. However, if she went out of business, there would be fewer dresses on the market. Would the price of dresses then go up or down? The question, she suggested, answered itself. So, we jumped to the Q.E.D.: that price controls had the effect of creating shortages and thus raising the prices they were designed to lower.

She demurred: "The government could go into the business."

And could sell dresses at a loss which would be made up by taxing the buyers of dresses.

"Can't enforcement agencies hold prices down?"

We traced the course of a pork chop from litter to the butcher shop, just to pick up the number of points at which prices would have to be fixed and surveillance maintained, not overlooking the hide's trip from slaughter house to the glove shop. Would it be wrong to estimate that the number of cops needed to enforce price controls in general would come to at least a tenth of the population? Would not the withdrawal of these men from productive work result in lessening the supply of goods? And, who would watch the cops?

"Well, then, are you in favor of the black market?"

We are in favor of the true market, even if it is labeled "black." The true market never can be suppressed. Even the ruthless Soviet commissars cannot do it. The students were surprised at this remark, so we related how, when the Russians reduced the value of the ruble, several years ago, they gave as their reason the large fortunes that had been built up by "profiteers"—which was an admission that an illegal market had been in operation. (Patronized by law-enforcement agents.)

"But, Americans are law-abiding. Didn't the OPA hold down prices during the war?"

They were too young to remember, and their textbooks do not record the shenanigans under OPA. How butchers would be "fresh out" if you asked them to weigh the meat before your eyes; how the tails of men's shirts were cut short to meet the fixed prices; how you had to buy an accessory you didn't want, at an outrageous price, in order to get an automobile at the legal price.

"If wages are held in line, prices would automatically follow."

Under wage controls, we explained, both employer and employee become criminals if one offers and the other accepts an increase in wages. During the war, to avoid putting everybody in jail, the War Labor Board hit on the device of up-grading jobs so as to make increases in pay legal. But applications for permission to increase were too numerous for the Board to handle, and the employers in desperation resorted to under-the-counter wage boosts, in order to hold their employees (so as to fill defense orders).

"You mean that neither prices nor wages can be controlled?"

Yes, they can; in the army or in prison.

III

"Wait a minute," the coed interjected, "I've got to take the affirmative side. I need arguments in favor of controls."

That was a chore. How does one support what one holds to be a fallacy? Well, underlying every fallacy is a doctrine, and if you accept the doctrine the fallacy seems to melt away. In this case, the doctrine is that political power can make the market place jump through a hoop; there are no laws of economics to hamper the strong arm of the State. We had to accept that position, if we were to be of any help to the affirmative side.

Sticking to the Socratic method, we asked: what is the advertised social purpose of controls?

"To distribute equitably whatever is in short supply."

Like the father, we suggested, who sees to it that none of his children gets more than the others. That is what we call "egalitarianism." To argue the affirmative in this debate, we said, you must accept egalitarianism as an ideal and a possibility; you must assume that the State has the right, the capacity and the duty to allocate production and equalize consumption.

"Hold on; you're preaching Socialism."

Maybe Statism, we volunteered, is a better word. But, why get disturbed over a name?

"We don't dare mention Socialism. The students don't like it, and neither does the faculty adviser."

Then we remembered that in the textbooks this controlled economy business is described as "democratic." Socialism is not mentioned. Putting nomenclature aside, we pointed out that the affirmative in this debate must rest its case on the goal of abolishing inequalities in the distribution of wealth and the State's ability to do so.

"What about the rights of the citizens?"

Pure fiction, we sneered. The only rights the citizens have are the privileges given him, on lend-lease, by the State.

"You mean the worker does not have the right to sell his services to the highest bidder?"

Of course not. We must keep in mind that the good of society, as determined by the State, takes precedence over the good of the individual. After all, if the worker insists on fending for himself, how can the State take care of his interests?

"But, surely, if a farmer has put his back into a bushel of potatoes, those potatoes belong to him and he has a right to sell them for whatever is offered."

It was the young man who brought up the right of property, and we had to argue that that too is fiction. In his textbooks, we said, he would learn that in our highly integrated economy the individual worker produces nothing; society is the only producer. If society produces everything, the State has a first claim on everything, and is entirely within its rights when it confiscates property (by taxation) and distributes it for the general good.

They were perturbed. This was hard to take. "You mean to say that to support the affirmative in this debate we have to take the position that the individual has no rights? That the State is supreme?"

That's your basic premise, we insisted. Once you admit that the individual has rights which the State must respect, the case for controls is lost.

IV

The students had come to us without prejudice. They were interested only in winning a debate, whichever side they took. But, when the argument for controls was related to the underlying doctrine of Statism, their sensibilities were aroused. The debate took on a new meaning; it was not an impersonal verbal joust; it was a battle of values, a contest between right and wrong—and neutrality was impossible.

When they left, we felt that freedom is not a lost cause. It is rooted in the human soul; it cannot be eradicated by sophistry, nor obfuscated by erudition. Once it is spelled out, youth will recognize freedom, embrace it and, if need be, fight for it.

CHAPTER 10

SOCIALISM
BY DEFAULT

WHEN YOU EXAMINE samples of the anti-socialistic literature which is flooding the country, you realize why socialism, despite its irrationality, is gaining common acceptance. If these booklets and "letters" were designed to aid the collectivistic cause they could not do a better job.

Taken as a whole, this literature can be catalogued as "Swell Country; no change wanted." It is reminiscent of Harding's normalcy, or of Hoover's chicken in every pot, to say nothing of two cars in every garage. The "line" is to blow up economic half-truths flattering to the status quo, with the hope that such evidence will squelch the socialistic indictment of it. This literature is more than futile. It must boomerang, simply because it dodges facts that are as well-known as they are unsavory.

If the run-of-the-mill American is as gullible as this literature assumes, and there is reason to believe that he is, there are nevertheless the lessons of experience which even infantilism cannot dull. Imagine feeding rags-to-riches syrup to the sharecropper who remembers being dispossessed onto the highway, or to his children who learned to hold out the hand of beggary. Then, there's the glorious tale of the penniless immigrant who rose to affluence; what can be the effect of this pap on the fellow who lived by the grace of the W. P. A. when bank bankruptcy wiped out his lifetime savings? What goes on in the mind of the mechanic who, on reading about the "overall picture" of national prosperity, or the tables of comparative wages, recalls the ten years of wage-less nightmare, until the war brought hypodermic relief? Even now, dulling the enjoyment of his inflationary comfort is the spectre of impending depression.

All this experience the anti-socialistic literature passes over lightly with figures, carried out to three percentage points. The inference is plain that the "poor ye have always"—and nothing can be done about it. It's fine solace to be labeled an "unemployable" or to be put among the "surplus population."

But somehow the lowliest of the species resents being a statistic. He flatters himself that he is a man. Whatever his intellectual deficiencies, his sense perceptions are keen; recorded in the memory of his belly is data the economists cannot get to. And that memory tells him that there is a lie somewhere in the pollyannish picture of America being presented to him.

The Unanswered Why

Sure, there are more opportunities for self-betterment in this country than in other countries. Telling him about it is merely rubbing in the fact that maybe he hasn't got what it takes, and that isn't soothing. He knows there will always be a Babe Ruth, a champion. Well, all he asks of life is a steady job as bat-boy in the bush leagues, and he hasn't found even that modest ideal always attainable. Why? If this is such a great country—*why?* Observation tells him that many of those who rise above the ruck do so by other means than industry and thrift. There's the rag-picker made into a merchant by the black market; the town ne'er-do-well who attached himself to a political mogul and became a cigar-smoking contractor; the arrogant and opulent union leader who was the most inefficient worker in the shop; the newsboy who somehow got licenses for the best spots in town and now mingles with the "best people." And how about the fellows who finance these "God Bless America" pamphlets? What's their racket?

Sure, the "average" wage in this country is a princely income compared to that of the Chinese coolie. What of it? The "average" American worker—whatever that is—produces more; well, if he produces more he is entitled to more, and why give credit to a "system" for the labor he puts out? According to the figures in this anti-socialistic literature he absorbs in wages about all he produces, and yet his eyes tell him that there are a lot of fellows who produce nothing, or very little, and they seem to get along quite well. Who produces what they have? He's envious, to be sure, but he's also sensitive to a wrong he cannot locate.

The socialists locate it for him. He never will understand their many-worded fable about surplus-value and the class-struggle and the glories of controlled economy. No matter. These fellows at least come clean; they admit the poverty-amidst-plenty incongruity, and in so doing they gain the confidence of the mass-man. Having gained his confidence, they find it easy to "teach" him the mysteries of their solution. Their shibboleths are plausible; they "explain" and they promise. He accepts their leadership.

The let-well-enough school, on the other hand, loses his confidence right from the start by denying the obvious. Their encomiums of the going order are suspect. Their arguments don't ring true, and their figures add up to a sum that doesn't square with experience. Hence, the lavishly sponsored literature of the anti-socialist camp, if it is read at all, meets with a contemptuous "so what?"

Leaders Who Lead Nowhere

It is not, however, the inadequacy of the literature that spells the doom of private property, but the inadequacy of the would-be anti-socialistic leadership behind it. It is inane, stupid, ignorant and, above all, lacking in integrity. With such leadershp the case for private property is lost.

Let us admit that in the shaping of social and political trends the mass-man is a passive factor. He serves only as a battering ram in the hands of the leaders he attaches himself to. Since that is the limit of his capacity, his inclination is to stick to the job of keeping himself and his race alive; if he ventures beyond that sphere, as in voting, it is for the exhilaration his otherwise drab life demands. Such opinions as he entertains, or can entertain, he acquires in pre-digested and packaged form. He must have leaders to think for him. Yet, because of the vanity which always accompanies mediocrity, the leadership he accepts must flatter his importance, must cater to his ego. Nor can this leadership be effective if it lies to him about what he knows, however it may lie to him about what he does not know.

This fact the socialistic tacticians have been wise enough to recognize. From Marx and Engels to Attlee and Wallace, due homage was always given to the "will of the people," although the shaping and direction of that will has ever been the private prerogative of the intelligentsia, the leadership. They won the mass-man by appealing to the intelligence they knew he did not have; in the name of education they filled him with phrases which served him well enough for understanding. But—and this is of utmost importance—he became a willing "student" because they told him what he knew only too well: that the world as is is NOT the best of all possible worlds.

Socialism has come a long way, then, because of competent leadership. The proponents of private property, on the other hand, have fought a losing game simply because of their ineptitude. The logic of economics is entirely on their side: it is only through private property that society can achieve abundance. Morality is also on their side: if a man is denied exclusive possession and enjoyment of that which he produces he is denied the right to life, and is in effect reduced to something less than a man. With these two arguments in its arsenal, private property should never have been put on the defensive. The collectivistic psychopaths should never have gained ascendancy with the mass-man.

But, the cause of private property has been championed by men who had no interest in it; their main concern has always been with the institution of privilege which has grown up alongside private property. They start by defining private property as anything that can be got by law; hence, they put their cunning to the control of the law-making machinery, so that the emerging laws enable them to profit at the expense of producers. They talk about the benefits of competition and work toward monopolistic practices. They extol individual initiative and support legal limitations on individuals who might challenge their ascendancy. In short, they are for the State, the enemy of private property, because they profit by its schemes. Their only objection to the State is its inclination to invade their privileged position or to extend privileges to other groups.

The Unassailed Citadels

It is what this literature does *not* advocate that stamps it for what it is. A few examples will suffice.

The current slogan of this effort to forestall Socialism is "free enterprise." Now, enterprise consists of nothing else, in the economic field, than the production and exchange of goods and services, by individuals acting in their own interests, and it is free only when the process is rid of legal interventions. The ultimate object is to provide an abundance of the things men want, to flood the marketplace. That means low prices, or prices determined by the equation of supply and demand without restrictions on supply. If that is what the "free enterprisers" were really for, they would concentrate on the rescinding of laws making for scarcities—and they would inform the mass-man that the cause for his lack (admitting first that there is an unwarranted lack) are these laws and the practices that have grown up under them.

First of all, they would direct attention to the scarcities resulting from tariffs, quotas, the manipulation of money, fictitious quarantine laws and other devices for preventing foreign goods from reaching our market. You see nothing about that in their literature. The inference is that free trade is not included in their concept of free enterprise. Why? Is it because of a concern for the higher prices which this limitation on competition affords them?

Taxation is a major interference with enterprise, simply because what is taken by the State is production which was intended for the market. Taxes on commodities are added to price and therefore decrease the purchasing power of wages; taxes on incomes and inheritances discourage production. These facts are rarely mentioned in any of the "free enterprise" literature; when it does touch on taxation the comment is limited to "equitable" distribution, which, on examination, simmers down to the shifting of the burden from one class of citizens to another. The reason is clear. You cannot expect the holders of government bonds to attack the income tax (which is the necessary precursor of State capitalism), because the prime security behind these bonds is the power of the State to levy on incomes. Nor can you expect liquor interests to oppose liquor taxes because if these were abolished every farmer could open a distillery.

You read in this "free enterprise" literature about government extravagances. But, what about particulars? Subsidies to railroads, airplane and shipping companies (via the post office) are clearly extravagances, supporting and encouraging inefficiency; but, the values of the stocks and bonds issued by these companies are enhanced thereby and hence the subject is taboo; subsidies which cannot be capitalized, like handouts to veterans and unemployed, can be attacked. Parity prices provide a cushion for the commodity market, and also hold up the value of agricultural land; the "free enterprisers" avoid the subject. Militarism is undoubtedly the greatest waste of all, besides being the greatest threat to freedom of the individual, and yet it is rather condoned than opposed by those whose hearts bleed for freedom, according to their literature.

One could go on paragraph after paragraph with instances of State interferences with enterprise which the "free enterprise" bilge skirts around or ignores. One is driven to the conclusion that the sponsors are not at all in favor of what they preach. They are rather for the status quo, for the legal setup by which they can continue to "enterprise" themselves into favored position. They are for privilege, as is, and not for the sanctity of private property.

Is it any wonder that the only following this kind of leadership can muster is what it can buy? Is it any wonder that the socialists have the mass-field to themselves?

CHAPTER 11

A WAY OF

DIVORCEMENT

IF IT IS in the interest of freedom that the Church and the State be kept apart, it is equally in the interest of freedom that the school be divorced from the State. That is so because it is impossible to immunize education against religious values.

To begin at the beginning, the substance of freedom is the right of the individual to make choices, without let or hindrance. That right is most highly cherished in the field of spiritual values. How we shall worship God, or whether we shall worship at all, is a matter we deem most private. For that reason, we insist that it must be outside the scope of political power; we know that if any religious order should possess itself of political power, it would be inclined to use it for the propagation of its dogmas and the suppression of others'. Nothing else can be expected, because every religious organization must logically consider dogmas other than its own erroneous, if not sinful.

So, then, it is to insure to us complete freedom in our choice of religious values that we have ordered the separation of Church and State.

Can we separate religious values from secular education? A religious value rests on faith. We accept it even though we cannot demonstrate it, because we cannot explain other demonstrable facts without this basic acceptance. In the earliest grades, the child learns that 2 times 2 is 4; that is true; but, what is Truth? That is a concept the philosophers have never been able to define, and in the final analysis we must accept abstract Truth on faith. The child could not get along with his education without it.

When the child gets to college, he is constantly confronted with basic acceptances; especially in those subjects that deal with human affairs: economics, political science, history, sociology.

II

There is, first of all, the question of "rights." Even the sixth-grader runs head-on into this concept. He feels—without understanding—that the teacher has invaded his "rights" when she shows favoritism. He hasn't figured out the origin of "rights," and he certainly cannot appreciate their religious character, as enunciated in the Declaration of Independence. But, without accepting the fact of "rights," independent of him and the teacher, he cannot make sense of his experience.

When the child becomes a sophomore he first learns that "rights" are merely permissions granted to the individual by a policeman, the State. If the sophomore should ask where the State gets the "rights" it hands out, or withdraws, he

might be told that the "rights" were originally deposited
with the State by the individual, on call. But, then, the question comes up, where did the individual get the "rights" in
the first place? There is no answer, except the unsatisfactory
one that the fellow with the big club gives or withdraws
"rights" at will, simply because of the club. And the residual
impression is that there is something divine in power. It is a
religious impression.

A more important religious value that plagues secular education is the one we call "natural law." When education
starts, the mother finds escape from the interminable "why"
by replying; "that's the way it always is." She's got to take
recourse to that vague acceptance after exhausting the
plausible explanations, like the stork brought the baby, or
the chair that hurt the child is a bad chair. Later on, the
teacher goes to "the nature of things" for her final explana-
tion; or, she might say, "it is the will of God." The final answer to all questions is an assumption.

But, the college professor is not so naive. He flatly declares
there is no such animal as "natural law," that it is just an
old-fashioned myth. The fact is, says the professor, that science is uninhibited by any rules of nature. Given enough
time, the scientist will figure out answers to all the unan-
swered questions. That, of course, is an unprovable assumption, and calls for an act of faith, in the infallibility and omniscience of science.

The rejection of the theory of "natural law," however, has
a very important bearing on our lives, besides opening the
way for a new religious idea. If, for instance, there are no
"natural laws" in economics—no fixed and immutable causal
relationships—then what's wrong with economic planning?
The all-important matter of making a living can be manipu-
lated to bring about any results you want, and nature be
damned.

To take another example, from the field of social science, those who begin with "natural law" will tell you that society is an organism that gestates, just like a baby, and you cannot do anything about changing the procedure. That is, society is not an artifact. On the other hand, the planning pragmatists come up with a Morgenthau Plan.

But, have we eliminated religious values—basic acceptances—when we reject "natural law"? Not a bit of it. We have simply replaced one unprovable axiom with another. "Natural law" calls for faith in an unchangeable pattern of things; when we drop that, we must have faith in something else, and that something else always turns out to be political power. Even the all-knowing scientist, in the field of human relations, finds it necessary to implement his wisdom with political power; it can do all that God is presumed to be capable of doing, and then some.

The point is, you cannot divorce basic assumptions—or spiritual values—from secular education. This fact, however, did not bother our forefathers when they put the State into the education business. In those days, not even the agnostic questioned "natural rights," and while the philosophers quibbled over the meaning of "natural law," it never occurred to them that freedom was in any way involved in this discussion. The religious concepts of freedom were so strongly imbedded in the hearts of our forefathers that they could not imagine the possible perversion of these concepts by the school.

III

The greatest phenomenon of the Twentieth Century is the rise of the secular religion of Statism. Just why and how it got going is not germane to this argument, but it is a certainty that the spread of Statism was facilitated by our schools. The votaries of this religion, whether by design or easy slithering, got themselves on the school payroll and, as evangelists have always done, went in for proselytising.

In the course of time, the students, indoctrinated in the schoolroom, manned the State; most naturally, they took their religious beliefs with them. So, we have a State religion coming in, so to say, by the back door.

Statism is a religion. It is a frame of thought based on unprovable hypotheses. Its primary assumption is that the State is a living entity, independent of its personnel. You can change the laws or the basic constitution, say the devotees of Statism, you can make a democracy into an absolutism, you can throw out the old crowd and vote in a new one—but the State is immutable. Mortals come and go; the State is.

The State, then, is supra-personal. It has an intelligence of its own, and this is not the combined intelligences of living men; it is *sui generis*. Even its ethical standards are unrelated to those of men. It is made by men, to be sure, but it transcends man.

Statism has its rituals, its prayers—"the State can do no wrong"—its hierarchy and its holy edifices. It even has the inevitable schisms and sects: Communism, Fascism, Socialism, New Dealism. The differences between them are ritualistic, in the main, and follow from the degree of power achieved; as between Communism and New Dealism, for instance, the difference is that in one private property is abolished outright while in the other private property is taxed outright.

Regardless of these schismatic differences, all the sects are agreed on the basic assumption that "divinity doth hedge" the State.

This is the religion that is being taught or insinuated in our schools, from the lowest grades to the post graduate courses. A junior high school teacher (in New York) is required to take her "social science" class each week to some municipal department and explain its workings. Her explanations may be objective, but the multitude of desks in the tax department, the magnitude of the water works, the complicated mechanism of the sanitation department all have an educational influence. The glory of the State is the constant obbligato of such teaching. (This, by the way, is a technique of what is called "progressive" education.)

And, the medical student cannot but regard with reverential awe the State that teaches him a trade and promises him a job—in the army.

Thus, a spurious religion, one that threatens our freedom more than any the Founding Fathers had in mind when they laid down the doctrine of separatism, has invaded our political institutions. For the same reasons that impelled them to bar the Church, the school should now be barred. In the interests of freedom, the public school should be dropped.

But, how? It seems to be an impossible operation; and yet, the legislature of South Carolina has inadvertently hit on a way. It has passed a law permitting local communities to go out of the business of education and to rent their buildings and equipment to private institutions.

If that idea were generally accepted and put into practice, neither Protestants, Catholics, Jews nor atheists would be compelled to support schools teaching the new, secular religion. The Statists, if they could find paying customers, could have their own schools, and be welcome. Every group would be free to teach whatever values seem best to them.

Under the South Carolina plan, the citizenry would be relieved of school taxes. Parents could then support schools of their own choice. And those parents who now suffer "double taxation"—support of the schools that furnish the education they want, and taxes for the other kind—would be in position to provide scholarships for children whose parents are less fortunate.

South Carolina has shown us the way to improve our educational system—a way that could lead us out of the clutches of Statism.

CHAPTER 12

JOSEPH, SECRETARY

OF AGRICULTURE

Long, long before Freud, a fellow named Joseph got himself a reputation as an interpreter of dreams. So, when all the Ph.D.'s of Egypt failed him, Pharaoh sent for this wizard and put to him the puzzler that had come out of his subconscious mind one night—something about seven lean kine and seven fat ones.

A biographical note on this Joseph is in order. Even as a lad he had shown himself endowed of special gifts, winning preferment in his father's eyes over a parcel of brothers. This aroused the envy and resentment of the fraternity—who probably considered Joseph a violation of the principle that all men are created equal—and they contrived to restore parity in mediocrity by getting him out of circulation. By devious circumstances he was landed into the service of Potiphar, a bigwig of Egypt, which was a long way from home.

One so clever could not be denied. He rose rapidly to head foremanship of Potiphar's estate. At this point, his career was almost cut short by the perfidy of a woman; that is to say, Potiphar's wife (probably a homely one who was "misunderstood" by her spouse) tried to seduce said Joseph, was repulsed, and, like a scorned female, framed her jilter. Potiphar dumped Joseph into jail.

It was here that Joseph came into his own. Among his fellow inmates were two who were bothered with dream problems. Joseph applied himself to these riddles and untwisted them with uncanny exactitude. This was remembered by one of the prisoners who, on his release, hired out to the Pharaoh household, and, when he heard that his master was deep in subconscious troubles, he recommended the diviner of the dungeon deep.

That is how Joseph came to be called to the palace. Realizing that an unpresentable psychiatrist is without prestige, he slicked himself up, even shaved off the insignia of his tribe, and offered his services to the troubled Administration. Quickly he came up with the answer. There was nothing to it. The dream, he said, indicated clearly that Egypt was about to experience the well-known business cycle, sometimes called "boom and bust." How did he know? The knowledge came to him by divine revelation, he said, which was far more reliable than the wisdom of the Harvard school of economics.

At this point, and while Pharaoh was flabbergasted into speechlessness by the positiveness of his prediction, Joseph showed his true mettle. He threw in a plan. True, he said, the seven years' boom was sure to come upon the realm, but the bust was not so inevitable; Jehovah could be cheated out of it by the simple device of laying up a reserve during the years of plenty. To execute that job Pharaoh would have to dig up a capable Secretary of Agriculture. The plan and the secretaryship had nothing to do with the riddle he had been called in to unravel, but Joseph tossed it off anyway, and was about to bow himself out.

It occurred to Pharaoh, however, that a mind that had all the answers ought not to languish in Potiphar's jail. So, on the very spot—confirmation by the Senate was quite unnecessary in those days—he appointed the surprised Joseph to be his Secretary of Agriculture. There being no Constitution to swear by, and no Bible to kiss, Pharaoh made the appointment stick by putting his own signet ring on Joseph's hand and a solid gold chain around his neck. For lack of an automobile, an official chariot was assigned to the new dignitary. No doubt, though the chronicle does not record it, Joseph must have a big office to work from, with a lot of assistants and secretaries, for mention is made of many overseers.

Henceforth, Joseph had no need to interpret dreams; he was an administrator, with a plan to carry out. Since the economy was completely agricultural, his position made him the real boss of the country, the top commissar. The first thing he did was to pass laws; without them no plan can work. And the first law on his agenda was, quite naturally, a tax-law. One-fifth of all that these profligate farmers should produce, during the years of plenty, must be taken from them and put under lock and key. It is reported that this 20 percent income tax yielded quite an amount; the grain piled up "as sand of the sea," and undoubtedly there was a shortage of bins, barns and elevators, for "it was without number."

In due time, as per prophecy, the depression came. It is not certain whether this calamity was caused by overproduction or underconsumption, and at that time the learned professors had not yet discovered the sun-spot theory or even the velocity theory of money. The magicians of that day were without benefit of postgraduate courses in economics. The tale, as we get it, refers to a "famine" but we are not informed whether the shortage was due to drought, pestilence or other unforeseeable accident, or, perhaps to the constant sapping of the economy by seven years of heavy taxation. From what follows in the story, it is quite possible that the dream-planner might have anticipated the consequence of his taxing scheme: the abject subservience of the Egyptian proletariat.

At any rate, hunger was upon the land of Pharaoh. And the people came to the Secretary of Agriculture and begged him to return the grain he had taken from them. Did he shell out? Of course he did, and at a price. He took their money, and when they had no more money he took their cattle. "And Joseph gave them bread in exchange for their horses, and for their flocks, and for their herds, and for their asses: and he fed them bread in exchange for all."

Still the hunger was upon the people, which was natural, for their capital was all gone, and without capital there is little production. As we know now, state capitalism had set in under Joseph's wise regime, and there was nothing for the hungry masses to do but apply for jobs to the state, at the only wage that it was pleased to pay, which was subsistence. They offered themselves as "servants unto Pharaoh" in exchange for bread. "Then Joseph said unto the people: 'Behold I have brought you this day and your land for Pharaoh: lo, here is seed for you, and you shall sow the land.'" In common parlance that means that he had nationalized the land and the labor of Egypt.

The dream-plan worked wonders—for Pharaoh and his Secretary of Agriculture. There is reason to believe, however, that some of the proletariat were perturbed over a moral principle: the right of a man to his property. The chronicle does not mention this matter, but it does speak of a migration of farmers from one end of the land to another, by Joseph's orders. Could it be that the slaves revolted? Could it be that Joseph resorted to the well-known migratory purge? There is no statement to that effect, but neither is there an explanaion for the shifting of the population, and in the absence of explanatory comment one may surmise.

On the other hand, it is told how a delegation of Egyptians came to Joseph and declared: "Thou hast saved our lives: let us find favor in the sight of my lord, and we will be Pharaoh's servants." Showing that the proletariat had come to terms with collectivism (since that was the only way to get by in this world) and were content with whatever security the Secretary would provide. Joseph, however, had to make some concession to private property, perhaps to encourage more taxable production; he restored to some of the Egyptians the land he had taken from them in their adversity, on a rental basis. The rent? One-fifth of all the annual output. By this well-timed act of policy, informs historian Flavius Josephus, "Joseph established his own authority in Egypt and increased the standing revenue of all its succeeding monarchs."

Though the succeeding monarchs and the succeeding commissars did well under the plan introduced by Joseph, it seems (according to later historians) that it put upon the proletarians a moral blight, so that when conquerors from other lands came to Egypt they met with little resistance; those who had nothing to lose had nothing to fight for. So that even the monarchs had to beg the invaders for administrative jobs. And lots of dust fell on the civilization of Pharaoh.

Four thousand years later, give or take a century or two, there was a land called America. It was ruled by a President, which was an office attained by a complex system of parties and votes. At the time under consideration the Presidency was occupied by a person called Harry Truman, about whom little was known except that he too had a dream: farmers who should wax wealthy without working, urban toilers who should feed well without paying.

Truth is, the dream was induced by intense political pre-occupation. Having been thrust into pre-eminence by the Democratic Party, a peculiarly fractious sect, he was in duty bound to strengthen and perpetuate its clutch on the tax-fund of the nation. Now, as has been noted, rulership in this land was dependent on votes. They were a strange people, these Americans, in that they loved to flavor their gross prac-ticality with the ambrosia of idealism. However, the fact remains they voted according to their gastronomic content-ment or disorder, as the case may be.

Well, the aforesaid dream perturbed the ruler of the Americans very much. He spoke of it often and loudly, espe-cially when he was pleading for another term of em-ployment. Finally he too called upon the Secretary of Agriculture, one yclept Brannan, to decipher for him this manna-from-heaven fantasy. This dignitary, it is recorded, replied: "It's a cinch, boss, I could bust this riddle on the spot, but I'd rather take a day or two to put the answer into protocol, for the sake of appearance, and to lend it a coat of erudition I'll call in a couple of fellows who majored in eco-nomics. Got to do it right, you know."

Shortly thereafter the Secretary handed the President a screed, which in those days was called a legislative bill, em-bodying not only the solution of his subconscious conun-drum but also a plan for putting its purport into execution. The dream signified, said the Secretary, that the farmers must be won to the sacred Democratic Party by assuring them of high prices for their products, and the proletarians of the cities by providing them with cheap edibles. "It can be done. All we need is a plan. I have it all here, in the form of a bill, and if you can get that do-nothing Congress to put the ok on it, you can leave the rest to me!" The President was pleased.

The first thing called for in the plan was an appropriation for an enforcement agency, which in itself would provide an easy living for a goodly number of loyal Democrats. That was fine. Then, a schedule of production would be presented to the farmers; in effect, they would be told when, how and what they should produce. Farmers who produced more than their allotments would be fined, those who complied would be rewarded with subsidies. This control over production would enable the bureaucrats to fix the prices, regardless of cost and demand. The city dwellers, particularly in the months preceding election time, would obtain their strawberries and cream at practically nothing, for which they would be grateful to their benefactors, while subsidies to farmers who did not produce would similarly bind them to the party.

Of course, there will have to be taxes, continued the Secretary, for how else can the scheme operate? "But, as you know, boss, the voters never associate gratuities with taxation. The farmers and artisans, if they mention the matter at all, will be told that the 'rich' pay all the taxes, and that will satisfy them. The checks we send the farmers will more than offset the distemper caused by levies on their incomes, and the housewife's glee at the low price of cabbage will overcome the chagrin of payroll deductions."

At first the Brannan Plan met with little favor among American farmers, who, though they had to rub along with an average of less than two automobiles to the family, were rather satisfied with "parity" handouts and were suspicious of any change in the status. A few years later, however, the depression came upon the country, and in quick order there was a mad demand for controlled production and for prices fixed by political exigency. The Truman dream, like that of Pharaoh, came into its own by way of a plan.

It goes without saying that the eventual outcome of the Brannan Plan was not unlike that of Joseph's. Once the overseers of the Department of Agriculture got control of the farmers and the lands of America, there was no way of returning to the regime of private ownership; there was no inclination to, for the farmers were quite content to swap the hazards of their trade for the subsistence doled out to them by the bureaucrats. The city dwellers, likewise, managed to live and have children under the regime of fixed income and regulated prices. Nobody yearned for more (except a few recalcitrants who were soon made to see the error of their ways), nobody cared for change. In fact, with aspirations limited, nobody cared about anything. And the American civilization went the way of the Egyptian.

CHAPTER 13

MISGUIDED

PATRIOTISM

THERE IS no questioning the patriotism of men who, like Charles E. Wilson, give freely of their talents, experience and energy to the political establishment. The motives of these businessmen are of the highest. Their wisdom is another matter, and even they must at times question it. In helping the bureaucracy to further its purposes, are they acting in the best interest of their country? Will their sacrifices make this a better land for their children to live in?

We must not confuse these men with the obscene and ubiquitous five-percenters, the hired hyenas of the business world who grin their way through the labyrinth that is Washington. In all probability the firms they represent are incompetents of the same moral stripe, managing to keep one step ahead of the sheriff only with the help of government contracts and loans. This certainly is true of those who shore up their rickety affairs by borrowing from the RFC and other lending agencies.

Then there is another kind of "businessman" who must be written off. He is the man of means who has given up on the American tradition and is "buying insurance" against future reprisal. Having accepted the trend toward collectivism as inevitable, this fellow "comes to the aid of the country" with substantial contributions (sometimes through foundations) to movements and individuals who, in his judgment, are on the "winning" side. His motives are as sordid as his thinking is shallow. He is doomed to extinction by the thing he is helping to bring about.

The wisdom in question is that of the capable and unselfish entrepreneur who, answering the call of duty, as he sees it, permits himself to be drawn into the Washington vortex, either as a stand-in bureaucrat or as an unwilling contractor.

The case of a reputable New York engineering firm is in point. It is unthinkable that this old and successful concern ever solicited government business. How it got into it is not public knowledge, but the fact is that it has become a "finder" for the bureaucracy. When an agency is confronted with a procurement problem involving technological know-how, it puts the matter before this firm, which in turn sets its operatives to the task of finding the available skill and equipment. If the existing facilities have to be adapted to the Government's needs, their extensive engineering knowledge is at hand. If finances are needed, a Wall Street connection is contacted, and since a government contract is assured, the financial problem is solved as expeditiously as the manufacturing problem. The bureaucracy has scored a hit.

Through such methods many an entrepreneur who might

be rendering a social service is sucked into the collectivistic maelstrom. Unwittingly, and in some cases unwillingly, he becomes a tool of the State. Refusal to cooperate is possible, but what with the suggested taint of unpatriotism, or extinguishment through lack of supplies, or the danger of reprisal, only the most intrepid idealist would buck the suave bureaucratic bully. The profit-motive is, of course, always present—who is free of it?—but the fact is that as the economy becomes more and more politically controlled the area of private initiative is delimited, and then the question is not profit but existence.

But what of liberty? What of America's future? The time has come when the American businessman, along with all other citizens, must face up to fundamentals, and without equivocation. Does one help one's country by helping the bureaucrat out of a difficulty created by the bureaucrat, or is one a better patriot by refusing to cooperate?

II

The bureaucrat is completely incapable of making a useful thing. He talks about the virtues of a controlled economy, but when it comes to making any part of the economy work he is helpless. He has no equipment for it. All his training has been directed toward the acquisition and exercise of power. He can fashion laws, make phrases, manipulate situations, lie convincingly, deal under the table of protocol. He cannot raise an onion or cobble a shoe. He is lost when his lust for power compels him to look into the practical problems of production. It is then that he calls in a businessman.

If the politician could do it himself, would he call in a Wilson? Why share the glory of achievement with his intended victim? Besides, the businessman has a set of values that is entirely out of place in the political world, and his presence there is bound to be irritating. His insistence on

results, with the least expenditure of effort and without regard to personalities, is out of line with the point of view that
the only result worthwhile is political preferment.

Because of this basic contradiction, it is necessary that
the businessman either adapt himself to the political cosmos
or get out.

If the businessman succumbs to political perversion, the
cause is usually his own naiveté. His unfamiliarity with and
distaste for political thinking invariably gets him into some
impasse from which he is incapable of extricating himself.
Perhaps he has said something that results in a "bad press,"
or maybe he has signed an honest report that is politically
unpalatable to some "higher up." He is bewildered by the
reaction; such a thing never came up in his career. At this
point, an ingenious "middle" bureaucrat—an entrenched
civil service operative in the higher echelon—soothingly
takes his superior in hand and leads him out of the difficulty. From that point on the businessman leans more and
more on his savior—and he becomes a politician at heart. He
sinks into protocol, lending his knowledge and talents to the
purposes of politics, and forgets about the job he was supposed to do.

If, on the other hand, he is made of sterner stuff, his position will be made intolerable enough to compel him to throw
it all up. The case of Mr. Wilson is illustrative. He was called
in by Mr. Truman when the Korean affair started. Everything was at sixes-and-sevens in Washington; under the circumstances, Mr. Truman could think of no way out but the
regimentation of private life—the only cure-all in the politician's pharmacopia. How to do it? He reached out into industry for help. Now that the "emergency" has settled into
regularity, the need for Mr. Wilson is not so urgent, and
those in the know have rightly predicted his resignation. He
has made enemies. No one, not even he himself, will know

exactly how this was brought about; but it is a certainty that he leaves public life with a depreciated reputation; the boys have seen to that.

Nevertheless, he has served the purpose of the bureaucracy. He has set up the machinery for control, he has created a lot of plush jobs for the gang, and he has taken on himself the onus for the whole business. He has made the Fair Deal bigger and better—just as the businessman in the thirties "patriotically" came to the aid of the New Deal in another "emergency."

III

What must be the end-result of the mesalliance of business and politics? Just as bad money destroys the value of good money, so the virus of political intrusion into the body economic must undermine its health and ultimately wreck it. Private enterprise must go.

In the light of experience, we cannot come to any other conclusion than that if and when Socialism or Communism or Fascism—the political control of our way of living—comes to America and wipes out our tradition of freedom, its advent will have been facilitated by the misguided patriotism of the capitalist. Roosevelt and his starry-eyed social workers hadn't the slightest idea of how to put their "more abundant life" into operation until management showed them a way: the businessmen worked out the details of the NRA and practical farmers helped organize the AAA. Likewise, the Fair Deal would have crashed on the rocks of ineptitude if private enterprise had not steered it to shore.

To put it bluntly: Communism will not be imported from Moscow; it will come out of Wall Street and Main Street. It will show up as a disease internally induced by bad habits, not the least of which is the growing practice of capitalists to come to the aid of the political establishment, in peace-time as well as wartime.

Putting aside that large element of the fraternity whose Americanism consists only of an immediate profit, and think-ing of those who consort with politics because they consider it their duty as citizens, we must lay the error of their ways either to ignorance of basic principle or shortsightedness in temporizing with it. The basic principle, derived from all history, is that government is a necessary evil, not a means toward a good end, and that any course that tends to in-crease the power of government must deplete the power in the people governed. That is, there is an unending struggle between State and Society.

The Declaration of Independence—which is the defini-tive expression of Americanism—recognized that conflict by stipulating the limits of government. "For these pur-poses men institute government," it says. And what are these purposes? To safeguard the "unalienable rights"—the rights that inhere in the individual by virtue of his existence and are derived not from his government but from his Creator. That is all. When government goes beyond this limitation it is a transgressor; so says the Declaration.

So then, true patriotism, faithfulness to the American tradition, demands a skeptical attitude toward politics. It must be presumed, *a priori*, that the politician's business is never to further the area of freedom, he has no interest in it, and that he is rather concerned with expanding his own area of activity. Hence, he must be kept constantly under sur-veillance. Cooperation with his schemes is dangerous to the interest of Society. The best the capitalist can do for his country, for his children, is to oppose intervention at every point, regardless of immediate consequences, and never to lend his prestige or capacities to the political establishment.

CHAPTER 14

CONSCIOUS
SCHIZOPHRENIA

IF PSYCHOLOGY lacks something in
the way of being a science, it has nevertheless enriched the
language. Take the word schizophrenia. That's a mouthful;
once the tongue has mastered this polysyllable the temptation is strong to use it freely, usually to describe an irrespon-
sible person whom you don't like. That, however, is gross
name-calling and does injustice to the fellows who are trying so hard to elevate psychology to a science.

What they mean by schizophrenia is a pathological condition of the mind; the patient suffering from it (although
they say he doesn't suffer at all, but rather enjoys his ail-
ment) finds it difficult to cope with reality and takes refuge
in a world of dreams. It seems that this slipping off the cliff

118

of reality becomes automatic, that the patient's mind is completely out of his control. His will doesn't function.

However, with apologies to the psychological fraternity, I beg leave to borrow this fine word to describe the mental apparatus of men who, by all the known standards, must be accounted quite sane, but who likewise periodically give the world they live in the go-by. In fact, these men must be designated as men of superior intelligence and above the average discernment; sometimes they are called the "intellectually curious." They, too, regularly drift off into illusionary realms, but unlike their pathological counterparts they do so deliberately and quite consciously. They do so, indeed, to retain their sanity, which is under constant bombardment in the environment in which they are compelled by the need of existence to live. They split their personalities, so to speak, between the real and the ideal because of an inner necessity. They are—I hope the psychologists will indulge this free use of their word—conscious schizophrenics.

The conscious schizophrenic (hereinafter designated by the symbol C-S, to save typesetting) can be described but not explained. He was not dropped on his head in infancy, his father may or may not have been a drunkard, his mother never spat into his eye. Mental diagnosis cannot fathom the tap-root of his capacity for distinguishing between principle and behavior, between good and bad, between the beautiful and the ugly. All that can be said of him is that somewhere along the road of experience he picked up that mysterious thing called values, by which he measures the ideas and practices of the social order he was born into; and he has a habit of finding that social order somewhat below his mark. His yearning for something better takes the form of either open criticism or silent resignation; in either case he finds it necessary to take mental flight to a world in which his standards prevail. He is an Epictetus, a Thoreau or a Nock, if he had the gift of articulation, or he is my farmer friend in Vermont who shuts himself up with a well-prepared library every fall. Then, again, he might be the successful stock broker who admits he is nothing but a croupier and finds it necessary to take an intellectual bath every evening lest he lose all respect for himself.

But, what is there in the make-up of this C-S that acts as a magnet for values? His peculiarity is accentuated by the fact that most of his neighbors are as immune as their quadruped brothers. You cannot dismiss the matter by inventing a word for it, like "complex"; that explains nothing. Is it a "complex" that causes the editor of a daily sheet to recognize the obscenity of his own headlines?

Nor can you toss off the C-S by labeling him "maladjusted." The fact is, he is so well adjusted that, if he has a mind to, he can squeeze out of the social order a larger share of the material things it has to offer than those who find it the best of all possible worlds. He conforms because it pays him to conform, not because he is impelled to it by animal instinct. He is the ex-soldier who knows that the "G.I. Bill of Rights" is an outright fraud, says so, and deliberately takes advantage of it to the hilt. The run-of-the-mill veteran may do the same thing but is incapable of questioning the rightness or wrongness of it.

I know a lawyer employed by the Internal Revenue Bureau who describes himself as a chaser of cheaters who cheat the cheaters; is he maladjusted because he recognizes a basic immorality in the work he is doing? (Or is he, forsooth, suffering from a sex disorder?) A successful practitioner in psychology—or is it psychiatry?—tells his close friends that the rich women who maintain his establishment could best be cured of their ailments with a scrubbing-board or a horse-whip; is he maladjusted because he prescribes otherwise, takes their money, and then repairs to a volume of Byron to save his wits? No verbal ingenuity can make a mental case out of the man whose intellectual integrity is a notch above his behavior.

The C-S reveals himself only to his equal, and without the aid of a psychiatric couch or a dimly lighted confessional. If you hit him as one who can understand, the advertising man will gladly tell you how he gets the stench of his slogans out of his nostrils by nightly association with the mediaevalists. The man of affairs who has just come from a session in Washington needs no other shock treatment; he rids his lungs of the foul air he has been breathing by a tour among his rare book collection. It is under the compulsion of his values that the union leader tells you, privately, how rotten his business is. But, only a C-S can detect one; the professional mind-healer, whose standard of mental health is conformity to an average, will never understand him. (By the way, does this fetish of happiness-through-conformity reduce psychology to hifalutin propaganda for Socialism?)

Sometimes the C-S lets his values get the better of his judgment, and then he teeters on the brink of real schizophrenia. It is when he makes the assumption that his values ought to be common property and decides "to do something about it." He becomes a reformer. His reason should tell him that the people he proposes to reform would have come to his values if they had been susceptible in the first place. They escaped contagion simply because they were immune. That being so, what sense is there in trying to reform them?

The best that a reform movement can accomplish—barring the use of force, which reforms nothing—is to give wider advertising to its values and thereby catch a few of the sensitized who somehow escaped. That is about all the profit the reformer can reasonably expect for his efforts, aside from the specious self-glorification of "doing good."

On the debit side, there is the inestimable harm of up-
rooting many from their comfortable ignorance. They were
far better off when they knew nothing about the values they
are constitutionally incapable of absorbing.

When you consider the futility of reform, to which all
history gives evidence, you begin to understand the C-S.
You no longer wonder why the rich man, whose private life
is adorned with virtue and culture, consorts publicly with
the official who (as the rich man will whisper to you) began
his political career as a collector of tribute from prostitutes.
Or, why many, recognizing the essential immorality of the
income tax, will go to all extremes to avoid as much of it as
the loopholes will allow, but will not raise a finger toward
the repeal of the Sixteenth Amendment. So long as the conditions permit the enjoyment of a double life, indulging
abstractions and principles in private while playing the
practical game for all it is worth, sacrifice is out of order.
Why should the professor of economics jeopardize his livelihood by refusing to teach what he knows to be distortions
of fact and theoretical absurdities in the official text book?
In the quiet of his den he reads the books that satisfy his
sense of decency.

And this, by the devious route of speculation, brings us to
Socialism and to Russia. When the privacy of property is
denied the privacy of conscience cannot be tolerated. Ideals
which do not conform with the prescribed "social good" are
obviously a threat to it and must be obliterated. But, the
C-S is by nature a non-conformist; ideals, principles, abstractions, values, insinuate themselves into his being with
little or no invitation on his part. He is a rare bird, to be sure,
and his habitat is everywhere, in the pent houses and in the
slums, even in Russia; he is as ubiquitous as he is rare. Under the repressive conditions of Socialism he is more likely
to rebel than where, as in this country, he can still indulge

his values in the privacy of his cronies. Hence, it can be concluded that there is a keener appreciation of freedom in Russia than in this country. The very strictness of surveillance is evidence that, even among the commissars, and even though it is unseen, there is a boiling pot of individualism in the U.S.S.R.

When, as seems inevitable, the U.S.A. is similarly turned into a semi-penal institution, and the C-S can neither enjoy the material things of life nor the luxury of his values, he will put his best foot forward. He will come all out for freedom, not because he gives a hoot for freedom in general but because he needs it to fulfill his own life. Every revolution in the history of the world was instigated by a frustrated individualist.

In the meantime, as the process of socialization increases in intensity and scope, you will find the C-S retreating more and more from the confining social order. The rich man will retire; the poor man will try his luck on a patch of land. Or, he will emigrate to the wilds of Brazil or Timbuktu. The first effect of Socialism on American Society will be the flight of that element which alone can give it cultural and spiritual tone. The conformist mob, entirely devoid of values, will take over and a low level of mediocrity will obtain. But, unfortunately for Socialism, the C-S will germinate even in its midst—he is that kind of bird—and will make trouble.

It is cheap moralizing to condemn the C-S as a hypocrite. Who is qualified by his own behavior to point the finger of scorn at him? Surely not the cleric whose pulpit rests on dollars the source of which had better not be investigated. Nor the reformer who profits by the very iniquity he aims to remove. Nor the president of a college plentifully endowed with privileges and monopoly profits. Every institution which enjoys tax-exemption is estopped from evaluating the status quo. And how many of us can truthfully say that not one cent of our income is unearned, or, to go to the extreme, would reject a wage, a profit, or a dividend, or a subvention from the tax-fund? The C-S has the good grace to know (and sometimes to admit) that his existence is steeped in moral squalor; his flight to intellectual decency does him credit.

What is more, this rare bird is a carrier of values which would disappear from our ken if he were extinct. He chirps of freedom, of culture, of decency, even though he lives by other means, and his song is good to hear. Besides, if he did not exist, neither would this book.

CHAPTER 15

NO PEACE FOR

JAPAN

OFFICIALLY, the tragedy is ended. The curtain raised at Pearl Harbor on December 7, 1941, was finally hauled down at San Francisco on September 8, 1951. The participating audience has buried its dead, dried its tears, drowned the horrible memory in its preoccupation with new and prospective wars. The Japanese War is shelved in history along with its many predecessors. Finis!

But, is it really all over? Somehow, one feels that the affair of San Francisco is a hollow promise, that the solemnly signed "treaty of peace" is but the prologue to more trouble. The exact language of the document is most unconvincing. It declares the end of hostilities, but avoids reference to the causative conditions. If these conditions still obtain, how long before another eruption will take place?

War is made by politicians. But, politicians cannot make war out of sheer cussedness. The social conditions must be just right and the economic conditions most propitious; which is another way of saying that when people find living difficult it is easy to incite them against a "foreign cause" of their troubles. People will fight to live. Therefore, since in respect to the all-important matter of making a living, the pact of San Francisco returns the Japanese people to the *status quo ante*, or slightly worse, then it is not a treaty of peace but a tired truce. Like causes produce like results.

To glimpse what is ahead for Japan—and for the rest of the world—one must read the treaty in the light of Japan's pre-war economy.

II

In the early years of the century, when the growing American industrial giant felt the need of a wider market, it turned to that vast and potentially rich area in the East known as China. To the commercial mind, China in those days embraced all the territory and all the peoples between Siberia and the lands to the south under domination of the British and French, and most certainly included Manchuria and Korea. This was one economic unit, teeming with customers who had plenty of raw materials with which to pay for manufactured goods.

But, though this unit was ostensibly free to do business with whomsoever it wanted, the Americans found the way to it blocked by the pre-emptory positions held by European competitors. To meet this situation, Secretary of State John Hay formulated and caused general acceptance of what became known as the Open Door policy. This was a declaration to the effect that in the Chinese market the various competitors were to be on an equal footing.

At that time Japan was not much of a competitor, but it

was coming along and was very much in need of the Open Door. This mainland was of immense importance to Japan's economy. Aside from contiguity, the area was rich in all the things Japan lacked. Japan has nothing to sell but her labor power, which is a marketable commodity only when it is congealed in raw materials, of which Japan has practically none. She must import not only the resources that labor power turns into desirable things, but much of the food that fuels labor power. This near-by neighbor had an abundance of both. Hence the Open Door, which for Americans meant an opportunity for expansion, was for Japan a necessity.

But, the Open Door did not solve her problems, for though she had the advantage of distance, Japan was not able to meet the competition of the Occident. America was a particularly tough customer. This fact may jolt our protectionists, who have always maintained that our high-priced labor cannot compete with the "coolie" wages of the East. Yet, the fact is that with a wage scale lower than none, Japan was unable to undersell the highest wage scale in the world, even in her backyard.

Wages, as everybody but a Socialist knows, are part of production. The higher the wages the higher the production. Conversely, when the level of production falls the wages come tumbling after. In comparison with his output (quality considered), the American skilled mechanic is the cheapest labor in the world, while the unit cost of the impoverished Japanese laborer put him out of line competitively.

Japan's low-wage level was the result of political domination of her economy. The level of wages is determined by the level of production, and political intervention in the economy always has the effect of depressing production. For one thing, political intervention means taxes, which is a siphoning off of the wealth of a nation and a discouragement of capital savings. No economy can attain or maintain a high standard in the face of frequent visits from brigands, in which class, economically speaking, the tax collector must be put.

In Japan the political establishment had long enjoyed absolute control of the economy. This meant that Japanese production was loaded down with taxes, and even though some of these taxes were channeled back into the economy by way of subventions, the net result was a general impoverishment; subsidies have the effect of creating work, of stimulating activity, of spreading money around, not of increasing production. Production begets production, and the only way to boost the general level is to permit the producer to keep, invest and exchange the output of his labor. This is, concomitantly, the only way to boost the wage level.

The Open Door could not redress the harm done to Japan's economy by her political machinery. Since the State never abdicates in the face of failure, but seeks to cover up its deficiencies with an extension of power, Japan set out to overcome her competitive difficulties on the mainland by militarily closing its door to the Occident. Successively, she took possession of Formosa, Korea, Manchuria and then sought a monopolistic position in China proper. Her economy did not improve; wages remained at the subsistence level.

The causes of war are too complex to be reduced to a simple formula. But, history indicates that the economy of a country bears heavily on the advent of war. American revisionist historians have come around to the thesis that the depression of the 1930's eased our entrance into World War II. If we were conditioned to an acceptance of war by our economy, it is a certainty the Japanese were likewise prepared for it. So, the war came and spent itself and we have a treaty of peace.

III

There is some fear among those who have studied the treaty that its terms present Russia, or its Chinese satellite, with easy opportunity to dominate the Japanese, thereby putting our military position in the East in jeopardy. If this is true, it is true only because the treaty in no way suggests a solution for Japan's economic problem. Save for the internal reforms effected by the MacArthur regime, Japan's economic position is even more precarious than it was before the war, in that her population is crowded into less working space.

Japan is still poor in natural resources. Japan still has nothing to sell but her labor power. And the neighboring mainland is still rich in raw materials. These are the hard facts of the situation.

Japan has other neighbors, including the United States, with whom she could do business, and in preference to China. China has had more war, and is therefore in less solvent condition than Australia, the Philippines, other countries on the mainland, Africa. But seeing how the nations of the world are going mad with economic isolationism, the likelihood is that Japan will find trading with them difficult, if not impossible. She will be confronted with the "dumping" argument—that she is bent on causing general distress by giving her goods away free! She will learn that she is a menace to the "high priced" labor of Indonesia. India's "infant" industries must be protected against this menacing Japanese giant. The sterling bloc will ostracize her. America will bolt its doors when a Nipponese salesman is in sight.

One of the great anomalies of our times is the urgency, on the one hand, for political One Worldism, and, on the

other, for economic isolationism. Even as the validity of separate sovereignty is seriously debated by international com-
missions, and pacts for closer political union are drawn up,
the various governments are erecting stronger barriers to
trade, and thus splitting up the human race into hermetically sealed and hostile camps. This contradiction can only
be described as international schizophrenia.

When the requirements of protocol are satisfied, Japan
will probably be invited to join mankind's greatest fraud—
the United Nations. And we can already hear her delegates
pleading for the supreme privilege of buying iron and selling toys, and humbly apologizing for her lack of food. No
doubt the plea will be respectfully referred to the proper
commission for study. Shall its report, in due time, recom-
mend that Japan solve her economic problem by practicing
birth control?

IV

The weakness and danger of the San Francisco agreement
is that it has no bearing on Japan's primary problem. If Japan ultimately drifts into the hostile Communistic camp
against the Western lineup, it will not be because of an intent to defeat the terms of the treaty, but because of the primordial urge of the Japanese to live.

If, as seems likely, Japan finds the markets of the world
closed to her, she will be most receptive to any over-
tures China may make. Can she reject them offhand? Even
though trade with China—or Russia—involves political en-
tanglement, or Communist propaganda infiltration, the risk
must be taken. To a man with a hungry wife and child a job
is a job; the boss's ideology is not hard to take with the
wages.

This should be evident, and it certainly must be evident
to the conspirators in the Kremlin. Gromyko's performance

at San Francisco may have had its purpose, but it certainly was not to prevent the signing of the treaty. For a sovereign Japan, committed by world trade conditions to poverty, and no longer enjoying a liberal handout from her conqueror, will be most amenable to blackmail. Will this lead to war?

CHAPTER 16

THE MYTH OF
THE POST OFFICE

*"Congress shall have power to . . .
Establish post-offices and post-roads."*

THAT'S HOW it all began. Out of that simple and definite Constitutional authority has grown, by ample applications of "implied powers," one of the largest monopolies in the world. Its 1946 receipts came to twelve hundred millions of dollars, its expenditures to fifteen hundred millions. These figures, issued by the Post Office Department, omit a number of expenditures incident to the business which a private concern could not omit without committing an act of bankruptcy. The Department does not charge against its income any rent for the land it occupies; any interest on investment in its plant and equipment; any depreciation. It carries no insurance account, since replacement of a destroyed building is met by special Congressional appropriation; new facilities are also provided by the general tax fund, to which no refund is ever made. The Civil Service takes care of employee pensions. And, of course, the Department pays no taxes.

Notwithstanding the savings effected by such account-ancy, the Department has managed to show a deficit in all but eight of the past one hundred and twenty years. The-oretically, the Department belongs to us, the citizens. Al-though our only prerogative as stockholders seems to be to make up the annual deficit, our self-respect should prompt us to make inquiry into the management of our business. Congress has recently made provision for raising the post-age rates. Experience leads us to predict that this increase in income will be accompanied by an increase in the defi-cits. What's wrong with our business? Indeed, is it a busi-ness?

The last question is the basic one. The regular issuance by the Department of meticulous operational statements is in line with standard commercial practice, and this gives the impression that the Department is in fact a business, an undertaking to serve the public at fees commensurate with costs. If that is so, we are justified in judging the effi-ciency of the business just as we do that of any commercial enterprise; that is, by its profit-and-loss statements. To such a test the advocates of public ownership, who point to the Department as a model of efficiency, object, asserting that the yardstick of efficiency in competitive business is not ap-plicable to a public service. It should be pointed out here, in passing, that any private business which is not a public service, which does not render service to the public, cannot exist in a competitive field, since loss of trade will automati-cally wipe it out. Whether or not a government monopoly is a public service is a matter of opinion, since its existence is not dependent on voluntary patronage. But, if the Post Office Department is exempted from the scrutiny to which a private business is subjected by the marketplace, then its claim to being a business is a myth. As stockholders we should be apprised of that fact.

The myth of the Post Office Department is grounded in a well-advertised generality: that which can best be done collectively should not be done privately. That, however, begs the question. Why is the transmission of private messages[1] peculiarly a government function? How can we know that public operation is superior when private operation is outlawed? And, if the postal business is best promoted as a collective instrument, must this instrument be implemented with police power, or could it be carried on by a private concern, paying for the privilege on the basis of bids and depending only on public patronage for its livelihood? These are questions which the deficit-paying stockholders have a right to ask.

Custom has so strongly imbedded the monopoly idea in our minds that the mere suggestion of a private postal system seems fantastic. Yet, it should be obvious that long before the Government made itself the exclusive mailman people communicated with one another. The king's couriers are presumed to have been the first letter carriers, but it is more likely that means of communication and picture-writing came at about the same time, long before there was

---

[1] The Government's monopoly covers the transmission of letters only, and a "letter" is officially defined as "a written message, communication, notice, or other expression of thought sent by one person to another, which is forwarded for the purpose of conveying live, current information to the addressee upon which he relies or takes action." The Department's document called *The Private Express Statutes* expands upon this definition to some thousands of words, so that all and sundry may know what constitutes the punishable crime of competition with the Government.

a king or couriers. Men write letters not because there is a mailman, but there is a mailman because men write letters, and they write letters because they are social animals.

The American colonists had been communicating with one another in some manner for nearly a hundred years before the British Crown thought of intervening. In England the postal service was the private business of the king, whose income prospered by the letting out of the privilege to patentees. Perhaps the prospect of revenue prompted the extension of the monopoly to the colonies in 1711. But there was another consideration, that of imposing on the colonists the cost of delivering official mail free. That, as we well know, is the franking privilege, and however we camouflage the fact, it is an expense which must be met by a tax on production; in 1946 this free mail tax amounted to one-hundred millions of dollars, about one-third of the total deficit of the Post Office Department.[2]

The Crown's intrusion in the private affairs of the colonists raised considerable havoc; they had not yet swallowed the myth. They recognized the postal rates as taxes pure and simple, not as payment for services rendered, and opposed the imposition both openly and by evasion. The Virginia House of Burgesses virtually nullified the law by threatening to fine postmasters who carried out its provisions. Meanwhile, the private business of delivering mail flourished, even advertised its services, while the official post office showed a loss each year until shrewd postmaster Benjamin

---

[2] From the annual report of the Postmaster General for the fiscal year ending June 30, 1946: "The foregoing tables do not include in the items 'audited revenues' the sum of $100,246,983, which is the estimated amount of revenues that would have accrued to the Post Office Department if the postage had been paid at the regular rates on free and penalty mail." The losses listed are (in round figures): 74 millions on penalty mail; 24 millions on free registry; nearly a million on franked mail; the balance, a little over a million, on free mail for the blind, free in county mail and differences in second-class postage favoring certain classes of eleemosynary publications.

Franklin turned in a small profit to headquarters in 1761.

Had it not been for the intrepidity of free enterprisers (some of them official postriders who carried a letter or a packet by private arrangement), the Continental Congress would have been hard pressed. Obviously, the British-controlled system could not be used; intercolonial communication, however, was kept going by ride-for-pay men with hardly any interruption. Paul Revere is reputed to have been one of them. The Continental Post Office came into existence by the enterprise of a Baltimore newspaper publisher who solicited private capital for the venture and organized from among the subscribers local committees to carry on the service. That is, the need was met by social, not political, action. A year later the Congress took over and then came the clause in the Constitution which made the business of mail communication a permanent function of government.

The habit of running a deficit was promptly acquired by the Post Office Department. Concurrent with this habit came practices which we label corrupt. It was not, however, the behavior of the officials that, at the beginning, can be so characterized; though the possibility of using the institution for political purposes was recognized from the start, the idea did not come into its own until Andrew Jackson made "to the victors belong the spoils" the guide of political behavior. The deficit-making practices of the Department find their source in the cupidity of the contractors with whom it must deal. It should be kept in mind that what we call a public post-office system is in the main privately operated. Even today the major part of mail transportation is done by contractors—ships, railroads, airplanes, trucks—and the principal occupation of the officials is regulation. In the early days, when senders brought mail to the post office and there was no local delivery, and no stamps to sell, the Department's functions were limited to laying down rules and regulations, establishing routes and hiring contractors to carry on the actual work. On the general principle that the public treasury is "ours," and that raiding it is sound business, these contractors did their best toward creating deficits. Their methods are imbedded in the system.[3]

The use of public funds for private gain began with the side-line postmasters. For political reasons the franchise generally fell to newspaper publishers. Since newspapers were not then admitted into the mails it was necessary for publishers to make private deals with delivery men, and it was quite natural for the one with the franchise to use it to butter his parsnips. The Department hired postriders by the horse and by the weight of the contents of the mail-bag; it was a simple matter to let "overweight" mail pile up in the post office until allowance was made for an extra horse. Stagecoaches were required to carry a given number of passengers with a given amount of mail, and if the business in either mail or passengers exceeded the agreement one or the other was left behind; the lower-paying mail suffered until an exasperated public forced the Department to revise the contract upward. Whenever a change of route was ordered, even if such change was to the advantage of the contractor, the contract was voided and he was allowed to make an "improved bid." Thus, device after device was conjured up to facilitate the annual deficit.

The art of milking the public treasury via the Post Office Department reached perfection with the advent of the rail-

[3] There is no way of determining the total loss in subsidies granted by the Department, for they are not outright bounties for specific purposes and so recorded. The practice is to contract for space or services presumably available, even if not used or needed. The mail not carried under such contracts has acquired the soubriquet of "phantom mail." At the present time, for instance, some losing airplane lines are arguing that they be paid by the airplane-mile rather than the ton-mile, meaning that they be paid for every mile flown whether the planes carry mail or not.

road. The oft-told story is as long as it is sordid. From a book advocating, forsooth, political ownership of the railroads to cure the inadequacies of the politically owned Post Office, we get the following:

". . . the government pays in some instances as much for the rent of a single car for one year as it would to build the car. . . . It has been discovered that in weighing the mails the roads have often falsified the weights. The weighing is done once every four years, and upon that basis the railroads are paid for the handling of mail. It has been discovered that during the period when the weighing is done all sorts of fraud were practiced. Thousands of pounds of empty sacks, bags of grain and in one case even a pile of lead pipe were shipped back and forth and weighed over and over again in order to increase the weight of the mails." [4]

Flagrant mismanagement in the Department, showing up, of course, in deficits, have led to frequent outbursts of public criticism and "investigations." The resulting changes in personnel, and even improvement in methods, did not eliminate the deficits. It then became politically necessary to explain them away by a logic chopping peculiar to bureaucracy. Public works, it was ascertained, are entirely outside profit-and-loss evaluations. Their cost is an investment in service, just like a household utensil. The public which "owns" the public works should no more expect a return on these possessions than the housewife does from a pot or a broom. "We" cannot make a profit on "ourselves." That would be like asking the left-hand pocket to declare a dividend in favor of the right-hand pocket. And what in private business is called an operational loss in a public business is not a loss at all, since the outlay is merely an additional investment in public service. By such reasoning the deficit acquires a new

[4] Carl D. Thompson, *Public Ownership*, New York, Crowell, 1925.

meaning, one just the opposite of loss in a business venture; it is a mark of "social progress."

This line of reasoning, now very common among planners, came upon the Post Office Department, the first of our social-istic ventures, gradually and as a matter of necessity. It was needed not only to explain away the deficits but also to support the practice of using Department funds to help out private business. From the beginning, everything that moves and can carry a letter has had a claim on the public treasury through the Post Office Department. The posthorse, the stagecoach, the ship, the railroad, the airplane—each in turn came to the Department for a handout and, depending on the political influence it brought along, got it. Each invoked the "general welfare" clause to support its claim.

It is the cost of supporting the private carriers that con-tributes most to the deficits of the Department and puts upon it a burden which makes efficiency meaningless. And it is a cost that cannot be eliminated from public ownership. Whenever the sovereign authority invades the marketplace, it is inevitable that what we naively call "corruption"— which is but the political means of acquiring economic goods —will pollute the economy. History is so emphatic on this point that one wonders at the persistence of the pollyanish hopes of public-ownership advocates; in the final analysis these hopes must rest on sublime faith in the miraculous mutation of human nature by public office. The partnership of privilege and politics is as natural as the marriage of men and women.

The same human nature which leads to subsidy-raids on the Department's funds also makes for the performance of duties which, in a private business, could not be tolerated. When the politics motive supersedes the profit motive, the direction and intensity of effort is completely altered. The office-holder's bread is not buttered by a customer but by a higher-up, and hence his natural inclination is to cater to the latter, not the former. The case of the Postmaster General is in point. Here we have the head of a business who is neither expected to have any particular qualifications for the job nor to concern himself with its management; he is avowedly put there as compensation for political services. From the head down, therefore, the mail business is only incidental to the main chance. How, then, can we measure performance by the same standards which prevail in a business which must serve the public to exist?

The Department did not attain monopoly status in one fell swoop. It is quite likely that in framing the post-office authority the Founders of the Constitution had monopoly in mind, simply because centralization and monopolization are kindred thoughts. But, the evidence is not conclusive. The *Federalist* disposes of the subject with one sentence: "The power to establish postroads must, in every view, be a harmless power and may, perhaps, by judicious management, be productive of great public conveniency." Such words as "harmless power," "may" and "perhaps" lend support to the view that the Founders were not concerned with monopolization, even if it occurred to them. It is a certainty that the early Americans did not concede monopoly to the Department, for the record shows that they used it only when it was a "conveniency" and resorted to private means when it was not. Monopolization came by way of improved police methods, not public demand.

In Colonial times the postage rate was fixed at six cents per letter, if it traveled thirty miles or less; this was graduated up to twenty-five cents for a trip of four hundred and fifty miles or more. A "letter" was officially defined as a single sheet of paper. If the packet contained two or more sheets, even if printed, the postage increased accordingly, and since the envelope was not introduced until 1842, post-masters could easily check on the number of sheets, which were folded and sealed. As the fee was paid by the recipient, neighborliness induced laxity in collecting the full postage. In 1799 the rates were raised, but this specific seemed to aggravate the deficit it was supposed to cure (because high prices drive business away or bring in substitutes), and in 1816 the rates reverted to the previous scale.

Unless people are acclimated to regimentation, their discontent arouses their imagination; the Americans of that time were not so acclimated and therefore they turned for relief from poor or costly postal service to hired messengers, traveling friends and the newly arisen "dispatch" and "express" companies that proudly offered cheaper and better mail service. The resort to social power was spontaneous and uninhibited. It became so customary to request travelers, even though strangers, to deliver letters to the towns to which they were going that merchants contemplating trips were careful to conceal the fact for fear of being inundated. Francis Lieber, a German traveler in the early thirties, makes this comment on the general practice: "I believe this is the only civilized country in which no law exists to prohibit private persons from carrying sealed letters. It would be considered a strange interference with private concerns if ever a law of this kind should be attempted here." [5] A strange interference indeed—in those days.

Now that "let the government do it" has become the litany of the land, this resort to spontaneous cooperation for the solution of a common problem, even one brought on by the government itself, smacks of heresy. Yet if we break through the socialistic incrustation of our thought, we will discern in this early Americanism a truth of political science,

[5] Quoted in Alvin F. Harlow, *Old Post Bags,* New York, D. Appleton & Co.

namely, that when political power is weak social power is
strong. The young government was too weak to prevent people from taking care of themselves. Not only did they resort
to mutual helpfulness in their extremity, but, and this is
more important, they took to the marketplace for a sound
solution. Commercial conveyors met the need for better and
cheaper mail service. The earliest of these on record was
begun in 1835, by William F. Harndon of Boston. Starting
as a deliverer of packages, he soon was employed to buy
goods in other cities for a commission, and it was but a natural sequence that merchants and others should turn their
letters over to him.

Where monopoly cannot prevent it, success is ever the
breeder of competition, and therefore of better and better
service. Harndon's venture gave rise to many more, and in
1843 Boston alone had a score of these operators, among
whom was Alvin Adams, father of the great Adams Express
Company. Merchants and others would club letters having
a common destination, delivering the packets to the express
company, or to a store which served as a collection point,
and for about fifty cents obtained a service for which the
government would demand as much as thirty dollars. The
dispatch companies maintained collection boxes in hotels
and other points of vantage. Hale's Foreign Letter Office of
New York published quotations on foreign delivery which
undercut the government's by about one-third, and in New
York it offered local delivery by special messengers at six
and a quarter cents per letter. It was a thriving industry,
this quasi mail service, growing with the needs of society.
Hunt's Merchants Magazine was well warranted in declaring
that "Government enterprise is wholly unable, under its
most advantageous promptings, to compare with private
enterprise." And political theory was not yet afraid of the
thought that "the transmission of correspondence is no more

a national concern than the construction of railways and telegraphs or the transit of passengers and goods."

One forceful fact emerges from the early history of the American mail. Private industry did not compete with the official Department so much as the Department competed with private industry; that is, the Department was forced to adopt or take over improvements in the service which the enterprisers introduced, lest it pass out from lack of trade. Before 1845 a letter mailed to one's neighbor bore a penalty of eight cents per sheet; the dispatch companies cut the rate for a single sheet and charged nothing for a second or even a third. That forced Congress to slash its rates, but the superior service of the private enterprises kept them in business nevertheless. What did the government do? In 1860 this pernicious social instinct compelled the Department to resort to the only logic known to officialdom—force. The Postmaster General, calling upon the law of 1851, declared the streets of Boston, New York, and Philadelphia to be post roads, thus making outlaws of persons using these streets for the transmission of letters for a fee.[6] After a little opposition and even open defiance of the law, the dispatch companies gave up the ghost and the citizenry were compelled to accept whatever delivery service the bureaucracy deigned to offer.

The private dispatch companies arose because of the inadequacies of the Department, and even though they were outlawed, there was always the threat of "black market" operations to keep the Department from backsliding. It might be well to recount some of the inadequacies which the

[6] This legal device of declaring lines of communication post roads is the prime means of monopolization; the secondary means is subsidies, making competition unprofitable. In 1813 the navigable rivers were declared post roads; in 1838 it was the railroads. Control of city streets came in 1853 with "free delivery service"; in 1896 rural roads were pre-empted wherever R.F.D. was ordered. Now it is the airways.

dispatch companies served to overcome. When the postage stamp was introduced in 1845 (five years after it was authorized), the purchaser had to climb to a sequestered cashier's office upstairs and wait his turn. Another ally of the dispatch company was the local postmaster, whose interest in city delivery was decidedly negative, since the rent of the private mail box was his to keep.[7] The post office was always located in an inconvenient part of the city, simply because the city regularly and rapidly outgrew the location, and the dispatch companies saved merchants the hire of messengers to linger on the long lines at the distant post office. It was not until the close of the Civil War that the tedious trip to the post office was overcome by the letter box, although this device had been in use in Europe for nearly two decades. That such conveniences would have crept into the bureaucratic channels eventually is a matter of conjecture; that the threat of social action accelerated their coming is a matter of fact.

It was pointed out that the postrider and the stagecoach were doing business before the Department acquired a proprietary interest in them by way of subsidization. So, too, did ship captains traveling along the coast and across the Atlantic carry mail long before they were invited to tap the public treasury, and the masters of inland river boats did not wait until the Department declared these waterways post roads in 1813. Despite the lack of a subsidy, the firm of Russell, Majors and Waddell started the famous transcontinental link between St. Joseph and San Francisco known as the Pony Express. When California came into the Union, mail was delivered only to San Francisco, at first by way of Cape

[7] This and other indirect emoluments were so considerable that Congress in 1845 limited the postmaster's income at $5,000. Until 1845 also, the postmaster enjoyed the deficit-helping, franking privilege on his private correspondence and newspapers.

Horn, later by the privately operated Overland Mail.[8] From San Francisco the mail was delivered to the mining camps and other towns by express companies, the most enterprising of which was Wells, Fargo & Company. In 1864 this company bought a quarter of a million stamps and envelopes from the Government and resold them with their delivery fee added. For some years its mail operations exceeded that of the Government in the West. Commodore Vanderbilt secured from the Nicaraguan Government a franchise for a transit route in 1851 and was soon postmarking letters "In Advance of the Mails." Charles P. Kimball, a San Francisco stationer, collected letters destined for the East, forwarding them via the Isthmus of Panama; from the habit of hawking his service on the streets just before sailing time he got the name of The Noisy Carrier.

And so the story goes. All the pioneering in the mail business was done by private enterprise. Some of the pioneers failed, either through incompetence or as a result of technological changes. Nevertheless, it is to their spirit of adventure, abetted by the profit motive, that we owe what we have of a mail service. Officialdom merely bought out what private initiative had produced and then legislated private initiative out of the field. What might have happened to the system if political monopolization could have been effected right from the start is horrendous to imagine. On the other hand, one can make comparison with privately owned communication systems to picture the kind of mail service we might now enjoy if the politician had kept his hands out of it. Putting aside such considerations as speed, economy,

[8] The way of the Post Office Department toward monopolization through its deficit-making power is illustrated in the case of the Overland line. John Butterfield, the operator, received from the Government $600,000 a year for two mail coaches each way per week; in 1859 the revenue from the mails thus carried was only $27,000.

and the variety of services provided by telephone companies, let us compare only the courteous operator with the kind of answers one gets from postal clerks. What a difference! Some of us can recall the crudity of the early telephone; nothing but the urge for more revenue turned that toy into an indispensable instrument of commercial and private life; dividends, not subsidies, spurred the scientific investigation and sharper management which resulted in lower rates and better service. And so, if the Government had kept its hands out of the mail business, the pioneers would have developed a mail service comparable to the telephone system, and the taxpayer would have been saved uncountable deficit billions.

How fortunate that the Government did not exercise its option on the invention of S. F. B. Morse! The first experimental telegraph line, between Washington and Baltimore, was built in 1843 at Government expense, but for some reason Congress lost interest in the invention and it went to private hands. Those who maintain that the mail service would not have thrived but for Government support should explain why the telegraph did thrive without it. The companies which exploited the telegraph not only paid their keep, but as taxpayers have helped to meet the annual deficits of the Post Office Department.[9]

Is the postal system—"our business"—operated efficiently or inefficiently? How can we tell? Efficiency is a standard of performance, and a standard presupposes a method of measurement. By what honest yardstick can we measure the performance of the Post Office Department? Without

[9] An interesting speculation suggests itself. If the Government had had the income tax at its disposal, making more deficits possible, would the telephone and telegraph have been allowed to develop under private guidance? Would it now suffer from competition in the package-delivery business of the money-order business?

such a yardstick any discussion of the Department's efficiency is like a debate on "how high is up?" It will not do to
depend on comparison with another nationalized system,
like the Russian, for instance, for while one may serve better
than the other, both are conditioned by factors which might
make for essential inefficiency; something like comparing
the speed of a horse having one lame leg with that of a
horse handicapped by two lame legs. If we point with
pride to past improvements in the service, we are merely
comparing a stagecoach with an airplane and are not determining the possible efficiency of the airplane.

A business is an undertaking to serve the public, and
whether it does so must be decided by the public, whose
decision as to the efficiency of the business is final and ir-
refutable. In making a decision, however, the public must
have a choice between at least two businesses in the same
field. That is, only where competition prevails can we have
a dependable yardstick of efficiency. Under such conditions
the decision of the public is recorded in the ballot booth
of the marketplace. Grocer Smith vies with grocer Jones for
the dollar-ballots, and, since the field is free of compulsion,
the winner will be the one who, all things considered, renders the better service. He receives in proportion to what he
delivers, and what he delivers is decided by competition,
not his own inclination. For the public, thinking always of
its own interest, votes for the performance, not the per-
former; in the final analysis, the public votes for itself. The
successful competitor will gain because of the service he
renders, because of his efficiency, and his gain is recorded
in his profit-and-loss statement. This statement, in a competitive field, is the objective and mathematically accurate
yardstick of efficiency.

With a privately owned monopoly the profit-and-loss
statement is only a partially true record of its efficiency,

falling short to the extent of its monopoly position. By control of the supply of services—which is the essence of monopoly—it eliminates competitors who, seeking to gain the favor of the public, would force its standard of performance to higher levels. Since the public has no choice in the matter, save that of going without, it takes the services offered by the monopolist at the terms he decides upon. His profit-and-loss statement is a record of the performance he chooses to give.

But, the monopoly is under compulsion to achieve a degree of efficiency by its desire for profits. It must produce. Its monopoly position enables it to predetermine its performance, and its profit motive drives it to produce the exact amount that will yield the greatest net return. This presents a problem in pricing, which it solves by the trial-and-error method. If the monopoly exceeds the predetermined level of production, the price will have to be dropped to entice greater consumption and the net return will be the same; if it raises the price, consumption will drop and so will the net return. Efficiency in a monopoly, then, consists in finding the exact ratio between price and output that will yield the most in profits.

The perfect monopoly is one which enjoys a complete control of the supply, leaving the public with no recourse except abstinence. Only for short periods, as during an emergency condition, can any privately owned monopoly enjoy that ideal privilege. Every monopoly is at all times subject to limited competitive conditions. There is, to begin with, the possibility of a technological break in its monopoly position; oil broke into the coal monopoly, the wireless took the transoceanic cable off its pedestal, the airplane made railroad management more considerate of the public. It is because of this threat that monopolies conduct expensive researches; and though the inclination might be to keep competitive inventions off the market, the existence of such inventions, and the possibility of others, is a pressure toward greater efficiency. Science tends to keep monopoly on its toes.

Other competitive threats have a bearing on the efficiency of the privately owned monopoly. The possibility of losing trade to substitute, even inferior, services is always present, while self-denial by an impecunious public is a constant consideration. That is, the public has a limited influence on the profit-and-loss statement of the monopoly.

A politicalized monopoly, however, is absolute. Every competitive influence is removed by force. Even abstinence on the part of the public is no threat, since every drop in revenue can be offset by a tax levy. The power of taxation removes the necessity of rendering service. Its profit-and-loss statement is meaningless as a measurement of performance; like the annual report of the Postmaster, such a statement can only be a pro forma, take-it-or-leave-it, memorandum. Since the public cannot take its mail trade elsewhere, the figures of the Department do not record the judgment of the public on the service rendered. Hence, discussion of the efficiency of the Department must be a fruitless conflict of opinions, loaded with preconceived notions and prejudices, not unlike an argument over the athletic prowess of Paul Bunyan.

The monopoly privilege of the Department does not cover all of its activities, and where competition is allowed, its inefficiency is glaring and definitely measurable. Its parcel-post business for the fiscal year 1946 shows a loss (not including unrecorded expenses) of forty-two and a half millions; its money-order business lost nearly twenty-nine millions; registered mail, insurance, special delivery, C.O.D. services, and postal notes lost another twenty-seven millions. Now, some of these services can be bought at comparable rates from taxpaying concerns, who seem to derive a profit from the operations since they advertise for trade. In these fields, at any rate, there is no question as to the inefficiency of the Department; it is definitely recorded on the yardstick of the marketplace. Is it unfair to assume that in the fields which it monopolizes the Department is at least just as inefficient?

If the claim of the Post Office Department to being a business is a myth, what then is it? It is a political institution. In its organization and operation it is essentially in the same category as the War Department or the Federal Bureau of Investigation. The revenue it receives is not payment for services rendered but is purely taxation. A plausible relationship between the rates charged and the costs is maintained only to make the tax levies palatable, but the final determinant of these rates is political exigency. Let us not fool ourselves. The price charged for the delivery of publications is a tax ameliorated by their capacity to influence public opinion, always a potent factor in politics. Third-class postage and parcel-post rates and rural free delivery came when the farm voter assumed importance, and not because of the arguments of the mail-order houses.[10] That inarticulate and milling mass known as "the general public" is taxed the heaviest by way of first-class rates simply because it lacks the political power of a pressure group.[11] First-class postage is like every tax on consumption; it is

[10] In 1892 the report of the House Committee on Post Offices and Post Roads contained this statement: "It is believed that rural free delivery will aid materially in stopping much of the growing discontent that now seems to exist among the farming population." A depression was then on.

[11] In 1946 first-class mail (including air mail) produced nearly 50 per cent of the Department's revenue, and showed a "profit" of $199,000,000. This result is partially due to the three-cent letter rate, which Congress enacted only as an emergency measure during the war. Thus, the fiscal problems of the Government, not the cost of the service, decide the price charged.

unavoidable, it affects the largest number of people and must therefore yield the largest revenue.

Finally, the claim of the Department to being a business is denied by its activities. No matter how varied the fields in which the largest business may engage, all must be related to the prime purpose of rendering service at a price commensurate with costs. This is not so with the Post Office Department. Under far-fetched interpretations of the original authority "to establish post offices and post roads" Congress has gone far afield. Thus, the Department has been put into the banking business and the express business; vast real-estate operations, road construction, building and operation of canals, development of rivers and harbors, co-operation with the police in the apprehension of criminals, censorship of the mails, guidance of public morals— anything which by full use of the imagination can be connected with the business of picking up and delivering mail comes within the scope of the Department. The purely political character of the Department is demonstrated by its activities in time of war. During the two world wars, the Post Office Department has been used for collecting war taxes, selling war bonds and thrift stamps, recruiting war personnel, dissemination of propaganda, censorship of mail, supervision of private telegraph and telephone systems. As an illustration of what the Congress may include in the postal service, it once considered a bill to put it into the employment business.[12] Thus, Congress may make of the Depart-

[12] The Department's *Brief History of the U. S. Postal Service* says: "Up to that time it had been aimed to make the Postal System pay its own way by balancing expenditures with receipts, but Congress in 1851 recognized the post office as a vital public service and adopted the policy of 'service first.' This policy has been extended down through the years until now we have the greatest business institution and public utility in the world, not for money-making but for public service." That is to say, in 1851 Congress decided to abandon any pretext of running the postal system on a business basis and to put it under the limitless blanket of a "public service." It is anything that can be used for political purposes, at any cost to taxpayers.

ment any kind of an instrument of State, and that means that it is a political institution, not a business. Discussion of its efficiency or inefficiency in terms of public service is therefore completely out of place.

CHAPTER 17

THE SOVEREIGN
TAX-COLLECTOR

WHEN the Union was founded,
political scientists were agreed on the axiom that the source
of sovereignty is the individual. It is from him that government derives its powers. This involves another assumption,
the one about "natural rights" inhering in the individual
by virtue of his existence or by divine gift. The two ideas,
necessarily related, emerged from the revolt against absolutism, resting its case on the doctrine of the "divine right of
kings."

Neither doctrine as to the source of sovereignty is prov-
able. The nature of sovereignty, however, is beyond doubt;
it is the degree of coercion that the government exerts on the
people; and this degree of coercion is in turn dependent on
the amount of the nation's wealth the government has at
its disposal. For the coercion must be exerted by men, and

153

men must live while they carry out the orders of the government. The police must be paid.

In short, sovereignty is a matter of taxation; the more taxation the more sovereignty. Conversely, the immunity of the people is in proportion to the amount of their wealth they can keep out of the government's hands. It follows, then, that the Sixteenth Amendment, which gives the government a prior claim on all the production of the country, puts the government in the way of acquiring as much power as it is possible for a government to exercise; that is, under our revised Constitution it is possible for the government to attain absolutism. The introduction of income taxation destroyed the original concept of the Union—as consisting of autonomous states, in which political power was a concession from sovereign citizens—just as effectively as if it had been done by a foreign invader.

The indisputable fact of the Sixteenth Amendment is its socialism; it denies the right of private property. Other taxes, particularly the indirect kind, are apologized for on the ground of necessity: the cost of maintaining the political establishment must be met by the citizenry, but the levies are made as painless as possible by hiding them in the price of goods. The income tax, on the other hand, unashamedly proclaims the doctrine of collectivized wealth. The State may take whatever it needs, as a matter of right; that which it does not take is a concession. It has first claim on all the earnings of all the people. A paraphrase of the income tax law would go like this:

Thus much thou shalt have for thy keep. Thus much more for the keep of thy wife; and for the nourishment of thy children, until they too enter into the service of the State, an allowance is made. Thou mayest also deduct for medication, if any, and for such expenses of thy business as are necessary for its continuance, and a percentage for thy favorite charities so as to relieve the

State of maintaining them. All the rest belongs to the State, as a matter of right. And, mind thee, these exemptions and the rate of taking the State may alter at will, from year to year.

Is this an exaggeration? There is nothing in the Sixteenth Amendment, there is nothing in the spirit of income taxation, that puts a limit on what the State may confiscate. Legally, all that is produced by the citizenry may be demanded, and the relationship between the State and its subjects, as far as property is concerned, approximates the relationship between master and slave. What makes the slave a slave is that he is legally denied the right of property, and the master is so only because the law permits him to appropriate all the slave produces. The substitution of the State for the individual master does not deny the economic substance of slavery, even though the State cloak its appropriations with eleemosynary intent; the individual master also takes care of "his people." The primary right of the individual to life is denied when his right to the possession and enjoyment of the fruits of his labor is denied; he who may not own may not be. And it is foolish to talk of a sovereign people without the right of property.

The Poor and the Rich

In the beginning, income taxation was eased into our *mores* by its promise to "soak the rich." It flattered what the people were pleased to call their sense of justice, which was only envy. Their concern was with tearing down, not with moral principles.

The opponents of the Sixteenth Amendment were equally devoid of principle, for they were quick to make compromise, since the first levies were low and the exemptions high. As was inevitable, the exemptions were regularly lowered and the levies increased, so that income taxation now falls most heavily on those least able to bear the burden. This consequence was unavoidable simply because political power is incapable of self-restraint and stops short only when confronted with vigorous social opposition. Since its power is in direct ratio to its income, the State could not overlook the pockets of the poor; the poor are the largest segment of the population and their aggregate income is the most attractive target of spoliation. "The Congress shall have the power," says the amendment, "to lay and collect taxes on incomes *from whatever source derived* . . ."—and in that italicized phrase rests the unlimited power of appropriation; nothing and nobody are exempt, neither the incomes of the poorest nor the incomes of gamblers, thieves and prostitutes. It is the unequivocal assertion of the State's lien on all the wealth of the nation.

The passion for levelling that insinuated the Sixteenth Amendment in the Constitution obscured the fact that this all-inclusive power of appropriation must in time reduce the people to the condition of wardship. Every strengthening of the State is accomplished by a weakening of the moral fibre of the people. That is axiomatic. Just as a bonded servant is dependent on the will of the master, so do people deprived of their incomes acquire the habit of charity; they learn to lean on the only propertied "person," the State. Dependence on the State, by way of socialized education, "free" medicine, unemployment insurance, public housing, gratuities and subsidies of all kinds, becomes the normal way of living and the pride of personality is lost. When self-reliance falls into disuse, it atrophies.

Moral deterioration is a progressive process. Just as a worn part will affect contiguous parts and bring the entire machine to collapse, so the loss of one moral value must ultimately undermine the sense of morality. The income tax, by attacking the dignity of the individual at the very base,

leads to the practice of perjury, fraud, deception and bribery. Avoidance and evasion of the levies have become the
passion of the country, and talents of the highest order are
expended on trying to save something from the clutches of
the State. People who in their private lives are above re-
proach brag about their ingenuity in beating the law. Putting all the tax-evasion devices together, they come under
the head of lying; sometimes it is legal, sometimes it is illegal, but always it is evasion of the truth. The habit of lying
grows by the practice, and a people constantly on the alert
for an effective lie in the making up of their income tax re-
ports must in time put little worth on truthfulness as a whole.

The political concept of a sovereign people, capable of
self-government, rests on the assumption that the people are
possessed of integrity, if not wisdom, and that they are free
to make choices in the light of their understanding. But, a
people inured to deception by the necessity of living are not
likely to heed moral principles in the management of their
common affairs; nor does freedom of choice have any meaning if the best they can expect from the management is a
gratuity from their confiscated property. The sovereignty of
the people is rather tarnished by their willingness to trade
their conscience; a "bought" election is hardly the free expression of an independent people.

Yet, nothing else can be expected; income taxation must
produce a slave psychology. One must live. Since the source
of doles, subsidies, jobs and economic favors of one kind or
another is the tax-fund, the party in control of it is their natural "choice," while the best the "outs" can do is to promise
a more lavish distribution and hope that the promise will
carry weight at the polls. That consequence of the Sixteenth
Amendment was unavoidable. If ever there was any validity
to the concept of a sovereign citizenry, from whom the powers of government are derived, there certainly is none now.

The Rationale of Robbery

Consciously or instinctively, the proponents of home government (or States' Rights) proceed from a philosophical axiom, that the individual is the only reality. He alone exists. Without him there cannot be a society, and without society there is no need of government. Society, in fact, is nothing but a convenient abstraction, a word describing an agglomeration of individuals cooperating for their mutual advantage. The character of society is but a composite of the characters of its components; it has no other. In short, society is nothing of itself.

For the purposes of society—that is, the improvement in the circumstances of its membership—experience has shown the need of an umpire. Since all the members are assumed to be possessed of the right to do whatever they please, provided they do not transgress the equal rights of others, it is necessary for society to provide a means of preventing transgression or of effecting restitution when it occurs. We give government a monopoly of coercion so that it can prevent coercion.

On the record, however, the government, which must consist of fallible human beings, is too often inclined to use the power vested in it for purposes not consistent with its appointed duty; it frequently goes in for a bit of predatory activity in the interests of its own members or of favored citizens. The only preventative is constant surveillance. There is no known "system" that will automatically keep the governing committee in line with its social mission.

This problem of surveillance presents a physical difficulty. The business of the members of society is the production of goods and services; this is demanding enough and leaves little time or energy for the supervision of government. It is necessary, therefore, that government be kept within reach, small, and completely dependent for its keep on the will of the body it serves. If it engages in activities too complicated for the citizens to follow, if it assumes to be an active agency as well as an impartial umpire, or if it achieves economic independence at the expense of the citizens, it will surely get out of hand; in that case it must become a burden and a hindrance. The evidence of history supports the conclusion that simple, small and dependent government is the only kind that can be watched and held to its social aim.

That, in a nutshell, is the reasoning behind the home government idea—or the American doctrine of States' Rights.

The income tax proceeds from, or finds justification in, quite the opposite premise, namely, that society is not only an entity distinct from the individuals composing it, but is endowed with capacities and qualities superior to anything the individuals can lay claim to. The collectivity may be a merger of individuals; still, the merger is a thing in itself, with a character of its own. This artifact of man is greater than its maker.

Once the fiction of a separate and superseding society is accepted as fact, logic has no difficulty in marching directly to the income tax and to the interventions that follow in its wake. In the first place, the fictional premise liquidates the doctrine of "natural rights"—of immunities inhering in the individual. That doctrine, say the collectivists, is an unprovable assumption; actually, they point out, the individual exists only within the framework of society. He is like part of a machine, necessary to its operation, but replaceable and therefore of consequence only as an accessory. The whole is greater than the sum of its parts. As a matter of experience, they say, what we call rights are merely the liberties that society (acting through its managing committee, the government) deems it advisable, in its own interests, to permit the individual to enjoy; when society finds the exercise of these liberties inconsistent with its purposes, it is entirely justified in withdrawing them. There are no immutable immunities.

Particularly is this so in the case of property. The individual may not lay claim to what he produces simply because he produces nothing by himself. Society produces everything; the more integrated the society, the greater the subdivision of labor, the greater the total production and the greater the dependence of the individuals on the collectivity. It follows from this line of reasoning that society alone has a vested interest in all production, and what the individual obtains through the system of wages and profits may be appropriated at will; he holds it in trusteeship only. The judgment of the governing committee as to what part he may keep for his own consumption cannot be questioned.

Thus we have the rationale of the income tax, if one is needed; in point of fact, the political establishment does not go in for rationalization, but exercises its power of confiscation on the basis of law and custom. But, the argument is implied not only in the confiscation but also in the government's assumption of duties and functions made possible by the confiscation. First comes the confiscation under cover of law; with confiscation comes power, or the means of employing policemen (as well as publicists and lawyers) to compel or induce people to do that which they would not do if left alone and in possession of their wealth; power feeds on power, and so we have the Welfare State, or the complete denial of the sanctity of the individual and the glorification of the amorphous god, State. The rationalization comes long after the fact of power has been established. It is the moralization of theft. It is the self-glorification that makes it easier for the thief to enjoy his loot and facilitates further looting. It is the justification for the exercise of power.

Open Sesame for Absolutism

Subtly implied in the Welfare State idea—in the intervention in private affairs made possible by the confiscation of wealth—is the concept of inferior and superior orders of men. Those who are in position of power are there because of either innate capacities or special training, or both, and are thus destined to look after the vast majority not so qualified. This is a modernization of *noblesse oblige,* with very little *noblesse.* In this country we have not got around to identifying the rulers with titles of nobility, but the public mind is fast becoming inured to the distinction between bureaucrat and taxpayer, between an aristocracy of power and a subject people. The inurement was facilitated by constitutional methods, by strict adherence to the forms prescribed for limited government. Nevertheless, the division of American society into ruled and rulers is as real as if it had been accomplished by conquest. The will of the people had to give way to economic necessity, and as the habit of begging for handouts grew so did the importance of the benefactor. We have come by absolutism quite without realizing it.

That the income tax was bound to transfer sovereignty from the people to a ruling class is seen when we look into the economic nature of the levies. It is not, as the title infers, a tax on earnings; it is a tax on that part of the earnings that might have become capital. Obviously, the State does not take what the earner consumes, it takes what he might have saved. Savings become capital, things used in the production of consumable wealth, like machines, railroads, buildings. The more savings thus invested the larger the capital structure of the community, and the larger the capital structure the greater the abundance of things men live by. What the State takes thus lowers the total productive capacity and, consequently, the standard of living. Dependence on the State follows as a matter of course.

Nor is this conclusion refuted by the claim of those who advocate State-capitalism, namely, that the State employs the savings just as the individual would have done. The primary purpose of the State is the retention and extension of its power, not the production of things; in the latter field it simply has no competence. The individual capitalist is compelled by the marketplace so to employ his capital that the consumer will buy its products at a price that yields him at least the amount of capital consumed in production. The private capitalist must render a desirable service or lose his capital. The State is under no such compulsion. If it puts the confiscated capital to productive uses it does so for purposes of political power; it is monopolistic by its composition, and if what it produces does not meet with public favor the public has no recourse; you cannot take your letters to a competing postal service if the State's is unsatisfactory. The price charged by the State does not include all costs, including depreciation of capital, for it can compel the consumer, through taxation, to make up operational deficits.

Deficits are characteristic of every venture in State-capitalism; so much so that the State is compelled to explain them away; every deficit, the Statists assert, merely represents an additional "public service." It is not correct, therefore, to compare a Post Office Department or a Tennessee Valley Authority with a capitalistic venture. These are not businesses, but are political institutions. Whatever "services" they do render are not what we demand of free capital. State-capitalism is nothing but the use of what might have been capital to increase the power of the State over men.

The Great Moloch

In this country, the State has got around to appropriating approximately one-third of the total production, with the promise of more to come. It has, therefore, become the largest single employer of labor, the largest single purchaser of goods. Its continuing absorption of what could otherwise become capital reduces the number of opportunities for self-employment. Under the circumstances, men are compelled to turn to the State for sustenance, and by the subtle process of adjustment to look upon it as their benefactor and guardian angel. Its predatory character is lost in the pyramids it builds, in the monstrous works for which there is no economic need and which serve only to advertise its greatness and its goodness. The disposition of men to resent political power is thus enervated. Sovereignty is thrust upon the State.

Well, then, since the commonality in America has accommodated itself to the doctrine of absolutism, what reason is there to raise objection? Only this, that in the long run the general economy must decline with the wastage of potential capital, and with the lowering of the economy comes a loss of aspirations and the loss of human values.

There is one ineluctable fact of human behavior that Statism cannot overcome: men labor only to satisfy their desires. They do not work for society, they work for themselves; there is no way of collectivizing desires. If for their exertions they get mainly monstrous dams and propaganda books, things they would not make of their own accord, their interests in laboring diminishes. The futility of it all dampens their aspirations. A meal and a mate they must have, but the marginal satisfactions, the things they can get along without, like baseball and Beethoven, are dropped in the difficulties of acquiring them. The values are lost. If the State, in its own interests, does supply these marginal satisfactions—the Roman State provided circuses as well as bread—the sense of achievement that heightens enjoyment is gone; one takes what is given, asks for more, but there is no appetite in it. The loss of interest in effort, in self-expression, is the mark of a declining civilization. And that eventuality the State cannot prevent.

If this is what follows from the channelling of the wealth of the nation into the political establishment, then true patriotism dictates an effort to put a stop to it. The repeal of the Sixteenth Amendment is the one thing we can do to save America from the dust-pile fate of other civilizations. That alone will decentralize and weaken the American State— and set up government again.

CHAPTER 18

THE MOST PRECIOUS
HEIRLOOM

Is WESTERN civilization on the way out? Some of our more lugubrious prognosticators say so, declaring moreover that the passing has already begun; the *coup de grâce*, they insist, will be World War III. If that is so, then we of this era occupy a grandstand seat at an historical tragedy that will cause much puzzlement for the scholars to come. What data will they have to go by in trying to put together the plot of the long lost—our—civilization? Will they be able to reconstruct its main *motif?* This is a speculation that ought to interest us, not so much because of any interest in future scholarship, but because it might help us to explain ourselves to ourselves.

What is "western civilization"? To which question there is an antecedent: what is "civilization"? Much of the gloomy forebodings rests on the anticipated destruction by the atom bomb and other instruments of death, so that "the decline of western civilization" suggests a wiping out of all population. That is obviously an exaggeration born of fear. If the world is to be destroyed, if all life is to disappear, our age and all that preceded it will hardly be a matter of thought; it will never have been, and whatever succeeds us will have to be a new genesis. But, it is more than likely that nature will defeat science, that despite the most thorough job of killing we might devise, at least one boy and one girl will escape, so that a new generation will arise to worry about what went on before they arrived.

When a civilization disappears all that is lost is an accumulation of knowledge; or, more exactly, the memory of that knowledge. A "lost" civilization is a body of ideas of which there is no record, or a frame of thought that once influenced the way people lived but has since been forgotten and has therefore lost significance. As with the impaired memory of senility, the past has no bearing on the present. Thus, as far as the Communists have been able to obliterate the knowledge and the values that obtained before their advent, the pre-1918 Russian civilization has been lost to Russia, even though records of it remain elsewhere.

No civilization is ever completely lost. Some trace of the accumulated knowledge of an age does seep through to its successors, if only through the artifacts it bequeaths, and no part of the world has ever been hermetically sealed off from the rest. Knowledge has a way of seeping through all barriers, of overcoming all exigencies. Though the debris of Rome buried the ancient civilization so deep as to bring on an apparently complete ignorance of it, known as the Dark Ages, some record of it found its way into the archives of the East, to facilitate the eventual reconstruction. And, above all, even on the dark continent of Europe some flickering torches were kept alive by intrepid monks, with a devotion that bespeaks an unquenchable faith in a renaissance. Now that a new "dark age" is being predicted, the story of these monks and their monasteries ought to be considered. Who will perform a similar office for the resurrection that must succeed the predicted decline?

Why do civilizations decline? Or, starting from the other end, how do they rise? The process of disintegration must be the reverse of the process of growth; hence, an understanding of the one is dependent on an understanding of the other.

If civilization is a body of ideas, it follows that it is the product of human thought, which in turn is stimulated by curiosity. A civilization comes because the reasoning animal puts his mind to the discovery of means for the improvement of his circumstances or the widening of his horizon. Since he is also endowed with the more significant characteristic of insatiability, he is never satisfied with one discovery but must go on seeking new gratifications for the ever-increasing number of desires his imagination conjures up. Out of the wheel came the cart; out of the cart came the railroad; out of the railroad came the automobile; out of the automobile came the airplane. On the spiritual side, which is another facet of desires, he invents an object of fear to worship, but soon finds that unsatisfying and comes up with the more solace-giving concept of a universal God of Love. When his primary desires are satisfied, his insatiable curiosity reaches out into what we call cultural fields, and he enriches his existence with music, art, literature, as well as with ideas that flatter his desire for self-identification, such as adornment and ostentation.

That's how civilizations arise. It is necessarily a graduated process. The will to exist precedes the will to live. Only after the problem of existence is pretty well solved does the human being discover in himself any interest in improvement; only then do the marginal satisfactions—baseball and Bach —lay claim to his thought. They are called marginal satisfactions because, if necessary, man can get along without them. Any old shelter will do for a castle in the beginning, but when his larder is full he starts hunting for such things as a rug, pictures, a clavicord—to say nothing of hot-and-cold running water—just to make the old place livable. A civilization flowers in proportion to the amount of thought and effort man can invest in the satisfaction of his marginal desires. It is an accumulatively productive enterprise. Obviously, any diversionary or destructive effort, like war, must interfere with the nurturing of a civilization; also, if the human beng is insecure in the possession and enjoyment of his output, he loses interest in reaching out for new satisfactions and civilization is retarded. Peace and what we call property rights, which are in fact human rights, must obtain for a civilization to prosper.

Contrariwise, when living is difficult, when mere existence is the sum-total of satisfactions one can hope for, civilization hasn't a chance. And, whatever civilization has been built up will shrink as men have to give more and more thought to the primary problem of life. Men learn to get along without —without baseball and Bach—and in due time they forget that such things engaged the minds of their forebears. Long before the political entity of Rome collapsed, the number of Romans who took the slightest interest in the culture of the Greeks, or who had any acquaintance with the learning of their own illustrious forefathers, had dwindled to a mere handful; the principal business of the mass was to keep alive, and that was so demanding that nothing else mattered. When the essential word of a language is "gimme," little value is put on the cadences of poetry. And, when that happens, civilization is on the toboggan.

That is the theory of the rise and fall of civilizations by which those who predict the fall of western civilization measure the current of events. For evidence, they point to Europe, where concentration on mere survival has crowded out the intense interest in cultural values that characterized its population during the nineteenth century. In America, they find a general deterioration of educational standards, even though there has been an increase in student attendance; the curricula of schools and colleges are loaded with functional, rather than self-improvement, courses, so that these institutions have become training centers for soldiers, farmers, clerks; they clinch their argument by pointing to the infantile literature which is popular in this country.

Those who have hope, have their rebuttals ready. But, there is one argument advanced by the pessimists that carries more weight than all the facts and figures they can corral. It is the fact that western man has given up on the underlying concept of his civilization: the primacy of the individual. Of that there can be no doubt. All that we call western civilization seminated in the idea that all things begin and end with the individual, that he is the be-all and end-all of life. "Nothing but the individual exists," wrote a nineteenth century philosopher, "and in the individual, nothing but the individual." This idea that the human soul is the only reality not only released the human being from fetishes but also placed on him the responsibility for his environment. Since in the eyes of God every man is king, it was up to him to prove himself.

Out of that tenet of faith came the philosophy of liberalism that is the mark of western civilization. In its political

expression it lodged sovereignty in the individual and reduced government to the status of a maid-servant. In economics it gave rise to the doctrine of *laissez faire*. In social
life it did away with the fictional castes. It stimulated man's
spirit of adventure and he reached out into all fields, in the
sciences and the arts, in industry and commerce, and the
sum-total of his findings is western civilization. The whole
came out of a philosophy, which in turn rested on a tenet of
faith.

The evidence is all too strong that the philosophy is losing
its hold on men. Among the erudite—always prone to clothe
popular thought-trends with philosophic phraseology—the
inclination is to sneer at the concept of "natural rights,"
traceable only to God; and the popular thought-trend, induced by the exigencies of life, is toward the idea that
before the individual comes the group. Although it has not
yet been phrased that way, the conviction is growing that
God made Society, not man. For the habit of thinking, out
of which comes the habit of living, is shaping itself around
the axiom that Society (acting through the State) is an entity in itself, independent of and superior to its component
parts; the individual is only a means, not an end. It is this all
too obvious liquidation of the dignity of the individual that
supports the contention that western civilization is on the
way out.

A civilization dies hard. It is not a body of ideas acquired
by a few inquisitive minds, but a way of thinking and living
that has become habitual among men. Hence, a civilization
does not pass out all at once on a given day; the process of
deterioration is as tenuous as the process of gestation. The
historian needs a date and a specific event to mark the passing of a civilization. The prognosticator suffers from the
same conceit, and he picks on World War III as the finish-

line of western civilization. The exigencies of that struggle, he argues, will require the abandonment of the individualistic premise on which western civilization is based; with that keystone gone, the entire superstructure must collapse.

It is generally agreed that the anticipated war will be fought along totalitarian lines. The battles will be between nations, not armies; all will be warriors. The individual as individual will lose all value, for all thought and energy will be channelled into the one purpose of preserving the State. The first person singular will become a linguistic atavism; every sentence will begin with "we" and end with "us." To be sure, the doctrine of "natural rights" will be abandoned in fact, as it has already been abandoned in theory, and the constitutional immunities of life, property and conscience will no longer be claimed. Within six months after hostilities begin, it is predicted, all the machinery of a military dictatorship will have been put into operation, including, above all, the means of suppressing dissident opinion.

Granted this eventuality, does it portend a continuing organization of life? Will it not be "for the duration" only? To which observation the prophets of gloom retort, how long will the "duration" endure? Even if military operations are terminated within a reasonably short time, even if one side is able quickly to impose its will on the other, the destruction of the world's economy, to say nothing of the explosive hatreds aroused, will necessitate a long period of world management by the victorious side; at least, the dictatorship will deem such management necessary. Or, as seems probable, if sheer exhaustion induces a stalemate and a truce, it is a certainty that both sides will start preparing themselves for another test of arms, which means a continuation of the dictatorships. In either event, the duration will be long enough—two or three generations at the least—for people to have acquired a new set of values and to have forgotten about the past. The habit of individualistic thought will have given way to a thorough adjustment to herd-living. Thus, the seed of a collectivized civilization implanted in our *mores* in the early part of the twentieth century will have been fertilized by the conditions of war—and that will be the successor to what we have known as western civilization.

The prophets adduce an historical argument to support their thesis. They point to the fact that the State never abdicates; it is constitutionally unable to do so. Its character demands that it accumulate power, always at the expense of society, and there is nothing else it can do. It is a beast of prey, without any means of sustenance other than what it can grab. When its confiscatory power reaches the point where it can and does absorb all the individual produces, above a bare living, the individual ceases to have any interest in production and then the State has little to live on; in that enervated condition the State is pushed out of the way by revolution and for a while the people enjoy freedom. But, that is a long-term process. In the meantime, the power acquired by the State during war—when fear of a foreign enemy reduces resistance to its encroachments—is never relinquished; each war strengthens the State and weakens Society. Following this historic pattern, the prospect is that World War III will completely obliterate the individualistic premise of western civilization and will introduce a long period of Statism.

The heart of a civilization consists of a body of values; its collapse means the loss of these values. Other casualties, like its accumulated knowledge and its physical appurtenances, can be counted by historians and archaeologists; but, buried in these observable ruins are the values of which they are but the expression, and the humanist of another generation, immersed in his own set of values, has difficulty in capturing them. What, for instance, did the Greeks of 500 B.C. really think and feel? What were their aspirations, their ideals? What pattern of thought motivated their manner of life? These are the difficult questions that a lost civilization presents to its successor.

To repeat, the key value of western civilization is the primacy of the individual; all the rest is but a manifestation of it. If World War III does in fact destroy this civilization, it will do nothing more than depersonalize the individual and reduce him to an automaton. The social organization will, as near as possible with human beings, follow the pattern of the ant society. The concept of inalienable rights, stemming from God, will be superceded by the doctrine of permissive rights, authored by the Great Leviathan. Since the first responsibility of the human being will be to the collectivity, operating through the State, the Judeo-Christian idea of a direct relationship between the individual soul and the Supreme Being will be untenable. The soul idea, in the new western civilization, will be a lost value.

Now, whether or not this is an exact picture of things to come, or is only the idle speculation of lugubrious poets, the outlines of it are all too visible to permit offhand dismissal. And the history of past civilizations keeps dinning its lessons into our ears. The thing can happen. The only question is, is this consequence of World War III inevitable, something ordained in God's plan, or is it, like the war itself, an evidence of human frailties? There are arguments for both theses.

For those of us who, while observing the panorama of our times, are concerned about the fate of the *one* value on which our civilization rests, perhaps because of a natural attachment to our offspring, the argument of inevitability has no weight. If the collapse of western civilization is determined by the ineluctable historical cycle, the living man cannot resign himself to it, but must work out his career in the light of his reason, his hopes and his ideals. The stars in the heavens tend to their eternal business, and we mortals must travel within our own specific orbits. After all, it was not an historical imperative that directed the pens of those who signed the Declaration of Independence; it was a force within each of them. And for those of us who still hold high the value of human dignity, our job, whether we like it or not, whether out of a sense of duty or an irrepressible inner compunction, is to keep polishing up this value so as to prevent its utter tarnishment. We must be the monks of western civilization.

The supreme task of the present is spiritual. We are not concerned with saving buildings or gadgets from the impending holocaust, nor even its precious literature. All the physical accomplishments of western civilization must take their chances along with human life. Some things and some people will escape. But, what will happen to the Judeo-Christian tenet of the primacy of the person? Will anybody remember that "only the individual exists"? In the darkness and the stillness of universal Statism, will it be whispered that once there was a world built on the faith of the human being in himself and his God? All we can do now is to mobilize our forces in a struggle against the total obliteration of that value—and hope.

ENVOI

F ROM time to time, people urge upon me the espousal of some program they are pleased to call constructive. Some say that reform of our monetary system is the one essential of a healthy economic, and therefore social, order; single taxers are convinced that all things evil will vanish with the shifting of the incidence of taxation from production to privilege; for the pacifists, the cure-all is the abolition of war. I have been urged to take up the cudgels for decentralism, while those who see in "world government" the hope for human happiness have tried to press me into their service.

Every one of the proposed reforms has something to commend it in logic, while the sincerity of the proponents makes one wish that they could all be given a chance. The fact remains, however, that each reform rests its case on the goodwill, intelligence and selflessness of men who, invested with the power to do so, will put the reform into operation. And the lesson of history is that power is never so used. Never. I am convinced, on the other hand, that all of the evils of which these earnest people complain can be traced to the misuse of power, and I am inclined to distrust political power no matter who uses it.

The only "constructive" idea that I can in all conscience advance, then, is that the individual put his trust in himself, not in power; that he seek to better his understanding and lift his values to a higher and still higher level; that he assume responsibility for his behavior and not transfer his personality to committees, organizations or, above all, to a super-personal State. Such reforms as are necessary will come of themselves when, or if, men act as intelligent and responsible human beings. There cannot be a "good" society until there are "good" people.

Date Due